The Echo
of Our Song

The Echo
of Our Song

CHANTS & POEMS
OF THE HAWAIIANS

Translated and Edited by
MARY KAWENA PUKUI
& ALFONS L. KORN

1982
The University Press of Hawaii
Honolulu

Contents

Preface

THE INTRODUCTION OF this book is entirely implied in the wording of its title. We think of it as a book of echoes, muffled echoes, because, as everyone knows, no translation of a poem can achieve quite the same results as the real thing. Just as an echo can never take the place of the original voice so a poem-in-translation, however much it may try to become a "reasonable" facsimile, can never take the place of the living poem, in its primary language, and as known to its native audience.

With this much admitted, there is another sense, perhaps more gratifying, an excuse at least historic, in which the plan of this book might be said to follow an echo principle. We do not, for example, include in our table of contents any excerpt from the *Kumulipo*, the great Hawaiian creation chant, which contains some of the most ancient traditions of the Hawaiians concerning their gods, the origin of the sky and the sea and the world, the sea's islands and their creatures, and the myth-drenched records of their human and divine Polynesian ancestors. What we offer instead, as in the *Birth Chant for Kau-i-ke-ao-uli*, composed only about 170 years ago, is a sort of nineteenth-century offshoot of the *Kumulipo*—another echo. The sacred infant whose birth is cele-

brated in this chant was the prince, second son of Ka-
mehameha I, who ruled over Hawai'i from 1825 to
1854 as Ka-mehameha III, and who lent his royal
approval to the first Hawaiian constitution.

Likewise, instead of choosing for inclusion chants
and dance songs involving more or less legendary
heroes of the fascinating but remote Hawaiian past,
we have confined our choices (with one supreme ex-
ception) to a group of nineteenth-century chants and
poems representing everyday life as lived by both
chiefs and commoners in the Hawai'i of that era.
The modern heroes we celebrate include Bill the ice
skater, Ka-'ehu the poet-leper, the stalwart members
of Mr. Thurston's Water-Drinking Brigade, along
with the romantic Prince William Charles Luna-lilo
(most recently commemorated in having a freeway
named after him), and his political rival and cousin
several times removed, King Ka-lā-kaua.

The reader may for a moment or two be a bit
puzzled by the order and arrangement of some of our
selections. It is easy enough to understand why we
have begun the sequence with the *Shark Hula for
Ka-lani-'ōpu'u*, the high chief of the island of Hawai'i
whose nephew, Ka-mehameha I, first unified the scat-
tered Hawaiian islands into a single Hawaiian King-
dom. But why, one may wonder, include chants and
songs from the Pele and Hi'i-aka cycle, commonly
considered to be among the more ancient of Hawaiian
poems in their ethnic and linguistic origins? Further-

more, why introduce these selections only after the opening suite of chants about Ka-mehameha I and his family and other comparatively recent figures?

The answer is simple. Our arrangement is partly chronological, partly thematic. We begin with the establishment of the Ka-mehameha dynasty of Hawaiian rulers in the late eighteenth and early nineteenth centuries. We end the chronological scheme approximately one hundred years later, after the death of Ka-lā-kaua, with the fall of the monarchy under his sister, Queen Lili'u-o-ka-lani, and the end of all native dynasties. However, within that span we dwell here and there upon certain chants and songs that because of their cultural significance, their special resonance of suggestion, indeed because of their symbolic importance to many Hawaiians old and young, should not be identified too closely with this or that particular period, century, decade, or year in recent history.

Thus, as examples of a central theme in the gradual development of modern Hawai'i, we have introduced a few translations of Hawaiian chants and songs that derive their substance from the Holy Scriptures. One such example is the hymn entitled *The Love of God (Ke Aloha o ke Akua)*, a straightforward paraphrase into Hawaiian from chapter thirteen of the First Epistle to the Corinthians: "Though I speak with the tongues of men and of angels, and have not charity, I am become as sounding brass, or a tinkling cymbal." Our reason for interjecting several compositions by whole-souled Christian Hawaiians is simply to remind the reader that there is a persistent Christian stratum in the subsoil of Hawaiian culture, in the whole pattern of the social fabric, running continuously through the history of Hawai'i for the past 150 years. The three or four Christian chants and songs have been disposed at the particular spots where they appear for reasons of taste and opportunity for reflection, for pleasure too just at this point, and for the part they play in opening up unexpected vistas; but not for any wish to associate the selections with a particular date or decade.

Our reasons for interspersing two separate garlands of Pele and Hi'i-aka chants and dance songs are more complex. Yet the same general principle holds for the prominent stratum of native myth and legend in this book as for the subordinate layer of Christian belief and teaching. Historically these two dimensions in the life of modern Hawai'i have existed side by side, cohabiting either quite cheerfully up to a point or, when not, at least tolerantly enough, for nearly two hundred years. Again, we have wished to impress upon our readers that when, in 1819, the Hawaiians themselves set about dismantling their old legal system, abolishing their most sacred taboos, even before the coming of the Congregationalist missionaries, they certainly did not at one fell swoop

abandon all their most ancient arts and mysteries.
Thus they did not virtually overnight (as they were
inspired to do with their wooden idols) overturn,
bury, or otherwise insult and destroy all their an-
cestral stores of poetry and myth; or their racial
repositories of sacred dance and festal song; or their
rainbow-laden memories of the hundreds and hun-
dreds of chants and tales they had heard in childhood
and learned—sometimes relearned—first from their
mothers or grandmothers or aunties, or, less often,
from certain exceptional and strange poetic-minded
men.

In any event, the old pagan "unwritten song" of
Hawai'i did not suddenly vanish with the coming
of the missionaries or with the setting-up of the print-
ing press and establishment of the earliest Hawaiian-
language newspapers. On the contrary, the columns
of the Hawaiian newspapers of the nineteenth cen-
tury seem to show that there was an important ac-
cession into newsprint of the Pele legends during the
1860s. Then there was another wave of intensified in-
terest in the Pele and Hi'i-aka cycle, as might be
expected, during the nativistic reign of King Ka-
lā-kaua and continuing into the 1890s and later. It
should be remembered that part of Ka-lā-kaua's
political design for Hawai'i was to rehabilitate the
racial and political pride of the Hawaiians and to
cultivate in them a deeper sense of their Polynesian
and Southeast Asian origins and affiliations.

It is a fact of profoundest significance that dur-
ing the 1890s, after the destruction of the monarchy,
popular interest among Hawaiians in their native tra-
ditions, especially their oral traditions in folklore,
myth, prose tale, and poetic song, did not suddenly
collapse or even dwindle away. Instead, for many
Hawaiians as for a few deeply concerned friends,
the chief surviving symbol of old Hawaiian civili-
zation, of their as yet undefaced land and landscape,
and now of their derelict Kingdom, became the price-
less still-living body of myth and legend concerning
the fire family of Pele, the ancient doings of her
sisters and brothers, the other gods of the Hawaiian
pantheon, and the possible prophetic relationship
of all this mysterious matter to Pele's children and
descendants and to their kinfolk today.

In other words, within the chronological frame-
work of this anthology, we have tried to distinguish,
and at the same time interweave, several different
strands of poetic tradition, two of which relate rather
to religion and to the world of the supernatural than
to actual events of recent Hawaiian-American his-
tory: the tradition of the Gospel on the one hand, and
on the other the continuing life of the myth-making
Hawaiian imagination. Nathaniel B. Emerson pub-
lished his *Unwritten Literature of Hawaii: The
Sacred Songs of the Hula* under the imprint of the
United States Bureau of Ethnology in 1909, a half
dozen or so years after annexation. His *Pele and*

Hiʻiaka: A Myth from Hawaii, dedicated "to Her Majesty Liliʻuokalani and Her Beloved Hawaiian People," was privately printed for Emerson and modestly presented and offered for sale by the Honolulu Star-Bulletin Limited in 1915. The old queen died at Washington Place on Beretania Street in 1917. Clearly, the fascinations and consolations of the Pele myth, and the unforgettable chants and dance songs enshrined in the worship of the hula goddess Laka, have somehow retained a shadow of their magic into the last quarter of the twentieth century.

Doubtless other questions about the selection and ordering of our titles are pertinent. We hope that the commentaries both preceding and following the poems will help explain major points and clear up obscurities. Our more general principles of selection do not differ essentially from those followed in other anthologies of poetry springing from a once-"primitive," yet newly literate, tradition. Throughout our collaboration we have been concerned chiefly with: (1) the poetic interest and effectiveness of our texts; (2) their role in revealing the qualities of the Hawaiian mind and imagination; and (3) their significance as documents illuminating Hawaiian social and cultural history.

Finally, and never as mere afterthought, we have tried to show how native poets of the immediate Hawaiian past, whose names when known are mostly forgotten today, celebrated not only their land

but also the life in and of the land: as if simply
by naming and "placing" old scenes and sites of
Hawai'i's familiar landscape, redeeming it as it were,
the potential fierceness of the world might come to
be gentled, so that sky, ocean, shore, inland forest,
volcanic heap, sunburnt plain, and winding stream
might go on forever, just as in the past, as man's
proper and potentially friendly habitat.

A. L. K.

Acknowledgments

IT IS QUITE impossible adequately to express our
thanks to all the friends and colleagues who in one
form or another have contributed to this book. For
their constant encouragement, knowledge of Hawai'i,
and practical assistance we are deeply grateful to
Eleanor Williamson, Dorothy Kahananui, Marjorie
Sinclair, Samuel H. Elbert, Ruby Johnson, Florence
Maney, Arthur King, and Shiho Nunes.

Ha'ina 'ia mai
ana ka puana

Let the echo
of our song
be heard

Shark Hula
for Ka-lani-'ōpu'u

T HE CHANT CELEBRATES the ancestry and military skill of Ka-lani-'ōpu'u (d. 1782), uncle of King Ka-mehameha I. He was the "Tereoboo" who, with his retinue, dressed in feather capes and helmets, accompanied by priests, idols, and offerings of food, welcomed Captain Cook at Ke-ala-ke-kua during the navigator's second visit to the Sandwich Islands in 1779, the visit which resulted in Cook's death.

Nineteenth-century writers in Britain and the United States sometimes referred to the great Ka-mehameha as "the Lion of the Pacific." A more apt emblem for him and for his uncle and other warrior-relatives would be the shark, as in this sacred chant naming various ancestors of Ka-lani-'ōpu'u who had acquired authority over shark-gods, or over other chiefs who could claim the gods' magical services. Not only the shark but also the cowry, squid, eel, wild goose, and the frigate bird (*'iwa*) were sometimes regarded by the early Hawaiians as *'aumākua*, beings half human and half divine who were bound by obedience to their keepers. Their assistance could become a precious family possession of a line of ruling chiefs, a restrictive right dependent on supernatural agency and power, a kapu.

The shark hula for Ka-lani-'ōpu'u hails him for
his power over a variety of wild creatures praised
for their strength, controlled courage, and beauty.
Through this dominion, the authority of his kapu,
inherited through a line of famous ancestors—Ka-
welo, Ka-lani-kau-lele, and Ke-aka-mahana—the
"Island-Piercer" Ka-lani-'ōpu'u holds the right to
wear the royal feather cloak.

🌼 🌼 🌼

Hula Manō nō Ka-lani-'ōpu'u

'O Ka-lani-'ōpu'u, ke kū o ke kapu o ka moku iāia,
I pi'i ke kākala, i kekē ka niho o ka manō,
Ka pūko'a noho a ka i'a nui o ka hīhīmanu,
Ke koa'e lele i uka, ke aku lele i kai,
'O ka manu kīna'u nāna i popo'i ka 'ale iki, ka 'ale
    nui,
Nāna i pani ka i'a kapu 'o Ke-pani-lā,
Ka manō kākau 'ōni'oni'o i luna o ka moku o Ka'ula e.

E ō e Ka-lani-'ōpu'u o hou o ka moku,
'O kou inoa ia, e ō mai e.

Text: Mary Kawena Pukui

Ka lālākea, ka manō keʻehi ʻale,
Ka niuhi moe lawa ʻo Ka-lani-ʻōpuʻu,
ʻO ka hōʻeloʻelo wela ʻole ia o ka maka,
ʻO ka umu ia nāna e hahao i ka ʻenaʻena.
ʻO Ka-welo loloa nāna e hoʻāliāli,
A ʻaʻā ʻo Ka-lani-kau-lele ka hiwa.

O lalapa nō ka lāua keiki
ʻO Ka-pū-likoliko-i-ka-lani,
A kau maka manō, o ka maka ʻanapa,
ʻO ka nanana i ʻō a i ʻaneʻi.

ʻO ka iʻa nui hīhīmanu,
ʻO ka ʻiwa kīlou kapu o ke aliʻi,
ʻO ka ʻiwa nui nānā au moku.

ʻO ka lau o Ke-aka-mahana,
I puka ke aka o ka ʻahuʻula,
Lohia a maikaʻi.

🌸 🌸 🌸

Shark Hula for Ka-lani-ʻōpuʻu

Ka-lani-ʻōpuʻu, the right to impose the kapu on the
    land is yours:
        the right of a shark with arched dorsal fin to bare
            teeth
        of a coral reef to house a great stingray

of a *koaʻe*-bird to take wing for the upland
of an *aku*-fish to leap and plunge in the sea
of a certain mottled bird, a swift snatcher,
     to pounce alike on the small billow and the
     huge
and the right to bar and baffle the pathway of
     Ke-pani-lā,
     streaked like a tattoo, sacred marked shark of
     Kaʻula Island.

Now answer us, Ka-lani-ʻōpuʻu, fierce Island-Piercer!
     This is your name chant:

You are a white-finned shark riding the crest of the
     wave,
     O Ka-lani-ʻōpuʻu:
a tiger shark resting without fear
a rain quenching the sun's eye-searing glare
a grim oven glowing underground:
     towering Ka-welo lighted it
         who caused Ka-lani-kau-lele, the Chosen,
         to blaze.

Their child was flaming Ka-pū-likoliko-o-ka-lani
she with the shark's face and flashing eyes
she of the restless questing gaze.

O Ka-lani-ʻōpuʻu, stingray as fish, man-of-war as
     bird

in stillness lurking or poised aloft in flight
O ʻIwa, you do unite with hooked claw the royal
    kapu.

Your sovereign sway surveys this island and
    beyond
    over the multitudinous children of Ke-aka-
        mahana
        by whose name you do inherit and wear by
        right
        the shining feather cloak.

~~~~~~

NOTES

koaʻe-bird: The white-tailed (*Phaethon lepturus doro-
theae*) or red-tailed (*Phaethon rubricauda rothschildi*)
tropicbird or bo'sunbird.

aku-fish: Skipjack, Striped tuna (*Katsuwonus pelamis*).

Ke-pani-lā: A shark-god of Puna, said to be so huge that
when he rose to the surface of the sea his back was higher
than the tiny island of Kaʻula, southwest of Niʻihau,
named for the red-tailed bo'sunbird.

Ka-welo: A warrior-hero of Kauaʻi who was a *kupua*
(demigod) and who performed prodigious feats of
strength and bravery—throwing spears, hurling rocks,
catching giant fish. Ka-welo's elder brother was Ka-welo-
mahamaha-iʻa, a great chief of Kauaʻi whose *heiau*
(temple) was dedicated to the king of the shark-gods,

Ka-moho-aliʻi, and who was himself worshiped as a shark-god after his death.

Ka-lani-kau-lele: Half sister of Keawe, father of Ka-lani-ʻōpuʻu; she became the wife of Ke-kau-like, ruler of Maui.

Ka-pū-likoliko-o-ka-lani: A daughter of Ka-mehameha I; literally, 'the conch shell burning in the sky'. It is possible also to interpret the name as Kapu-likoliko-o-ka-lani 'the chiefess with the burning kapu'.

Ke-aka-mahana: Great-grandmother of Ka-lani-ʻōpuʻu, a ruling chiefess of Kona; a kapu chiefess descended from Lono-i-kamakahiki of the royal line of Hawaiʻi and also from royal chiefs of Kauaʻi. She was thus an illustrious female ancestor of all five members of the Ka-mehameha dynasty who successively ruled the Hawaiian Kingdom for more than seventy years.

Chant of Welcome
for Ka-mehameha

THE CHANT is the formal greeting of a chiefess
expressing her loyalty to Ka-mehameha I (175?–
1819), who by 1810 had "hooked" the islands of
the Hawaiian chain together into a single kingdom.
The composer-chanter was the high chiefess Ulu-lani
of Hilo, Hawai'i, remembered as the mother of the
defiant Christian convert, Ka-pi'o-lani, who in 1824
demonstrated her rejection of traditional Hawaiian
beliefs by repudiating the power of the fire goddess
Pele.

In Ulu-lani's chant of welcome she urges the Con-
queror to scorn the inhospitable people of Ka'ū dis-
trict as stubborn clansmen and near-rebels: for, like
"the rain of Ha'ao as it flies" over their bleak and
windy homeland, the Ka'ū folk continue to grieve in
loyal memory of their beloved dead chief, Keoua
Kū-'ahu-'ula, son of Ka-lani-'ōpu'u and own cousin
of Ka-mehameha, killed in battle by Ka-mehameha's
forces in 1791.

❀ ❀ ❀

He Mele Aloha nō Ka-mehameha

'O 'oe ia e Kalani nui Mehameha,
E hea aku ana i ka 'iwa kīlou moku la,
E ko———mo!

'A'ole i wehewehena, 'a'ole i waihona kona pō,
O ka hō'ā keia e——— .

A'u lei o ka ua Hā'ao e lele a'e ana mauka o 'Au'au-
    lele,
E komo i ka hale o ke aloha lani,
'Au'au i ke ki'o wai kapu o Pōnaha-ke-one,
E inu i ka 'awa a Kāne i kanu ai i Hawai'i.

Ola ia kini akua iā 'oe.

❀ ❀ ❀

Chant of Welcome for Ka-mehameha

You, O heavenly chief, Ka-mehameha,
great warrior, hero who hooked the islands together,
you we greet in welcome: "Come in!"

Text: Mary Kawena Pukui. Title assigned.

Dawn has not begun to break, night has not departed,
torches still burn.

Beloved ruler, leave the rain of Hā‘ao as it flies
    above ‘Au‘au-lele,
enter the home of a people who love their chief.
Bathe in the sacred pool of Pōnaha-ke-one.
Drink the *‘awa* planted by Kāne in Hawai‘i.

You are an emblem of life, a tribute to gods.

NOTES

‘Au‘au-lele: 'Flying raindrops', name of upland above
Wai-o-hinu in Ka‘ū.

Pōnaha-ke-one: 'Sandy circle', a bathing pool in Hilo. Its
location is unknown today, probably because many such
small springs and sea pools on major islands have been
filled with town refuse, plantation trash, and other waste
materials.

‘awa: A drink used in Polynesian ceremonies, as in the
worship of Kāne. It is made of the root of a shrub, the kava
(*Piper methysticum*), native to many Pacific islands.

Kāne: The leading god among the great gods; a god of
creation and the ancestor of chiefs and commoners.

Birth Chant for
Kau-i-ke-ao-uli

THE CHANT WAS composed in honor of a new-
born son of Ka-mehameha I, Kau-i-ke-ao-uli (1813–
1854), who, as Ka-mehameha III, succeeded his
brother, Liholiho, to the Hawaiian throne in 1824.
He was born seven years before the arrival in 1820
of the first New England missionaries.

The chant reflects conventions of the sacred art of
the hula, which has been described as "in essence
a magical ritual designed to bring rain and fertility"
(Handy, *Cultural Revolution*, p. 12). In pre-
Christian Hawai'i hula troupes, attached to the
houses of ruling chiefs, performed their ritual pray-
ers, songs, dances, and musical accompaniments
primarily for two purposes and on two occasions.
One was the annual *makahiki* festival, a first-fruits
celebration beginning in October and lasting four
months, in honor of the agricultural and fishing god
Lono. The purpose of the other occasion, as in this
chant for the infant Kau-i-ke-ao-uli, was to bring
"an enriching and empowering magic" to the cere-
monial and sexual union of *ali'i*, high chiefs, espe-
cially to the birth of a royal child destined to become
a great leader (Handy, *Cultural Revolution*, p. 12).

Kau-i-ke-ao-uli, second son of Ka-mehameha I
and the royal chiefess Ke-ōpū-o-lani, was stillborn,
a circumstance alluded to in the repeated references
to his mother's difficult labor. The babe was "prayed
into life" by a high priest, Ka-malo-'ihi (also called
Ka-pihe), whose therapeutic and prophetic prayer
made much of the idea that "the heavens will come
down"—in other words, that the native temples would
be destroyed, that their priests would abandon or be
forced from their priesthood, while the ruling chiefs
themselves would lose their posts as sacred heads
of government. They would become more like or-
dinary men.

In the birth chant of Kau-i-ke-ao-uli, in the re-
peated query "Who shall be here below?" there is
perhaps a pervasive premonition of this same notion
of the declension of the heavens and the transforma-
tion of the old ruling chiefs into mere human beings.

The name of the royal child, Kau-i-ke-ao-uli, mean-
ing 'placed in the dark sky', is expressive of many of
the thoughts obscurely, and yet so radiantly, em-
bedded in the language of the original Hawaiian.
The native word *ao* carried profound associations
for the early Islanders. The word can mean sky,
light, day, daylight, and dawn. It can refer to the
regaining of consciousness, and to achieving mental
enlightenment. The idea of dawn is closely connected
with the idea of night, and both fit in with the Ha-
waiian time sense, so that in this ancient language it is

quite possible to speak of "that night that dawned yesterday." In some contexts *ao* can mean world or earth; and it can refer also to any kind of cloud.

So in this single nuclear element of Kau-i-ke-ao-uli's sacred name are clustered and concentrated the seeds of some of the major symbols and sweeping cosmological conceptions found in the language of this old noble poem.

❀ ❀ ❀

Mele Hānau nō Kau-i-ke-ao-uli

I

O hānau a hua Kalani,
O ho'onā kū i luna,
O momoe o ma'ule ka piko,
O kolokolo ia pō ke ēwe,
O mulea, o malahia ka nalu, ke a'a.
O ho'onā kū o ka malama,
O ka'ahē a ka 'īloli,
O ho'owiliwili e hānau Kalani.
'O ia ho'i, 'o Kalani, hānau Kalani.

'O Kalani ia ho'i auane'i kō luna nei la.
'O wai la ho'i auane'i kō lalo la?

O hānau ka honua, a mole ka honua.
O kolokolo ka a'a, ka weli o ka honua.

Text: Mary Kawena Pukui

O lani weli ka honua, o lani ʻiʻī.
O holo pu ka mole, o ʻuʻina ke aʻa,
O hale ka pou lewa ka honua.
O pali nuʻu ka honua, ākea ka honua,
O honua kū, o honua noho ka honua,
O honua lewa, o honua paʻa, ka honua,
Ka honua ilalo, ilalo nuʻu ka honua.
O honua a Kea, nā Kea ka honua.
O honua a Papa, nā Papa ka honua,
ʻO ka hiapo honua a Papa i hānau.
ʻO ia hoʻi, ʻo ka honua, hānau ka honua.

ʻO ka honua la hoʻi kō lalo nei.
ʻO wai la hoʻi auaneʻi kō luna la?

II
O hānau ka pō iluna,
Hānau ka pō i luna nei.
O lani hāneʻe ka pō, o pīnaʻi ke ēwe.
O pipili ka pō, o moe anana leʻa,
O kōhi ana, leʻa ka pō o Mahina-leʻa.
O huli ka pō, o kaʻawale ka pili.
ʻO ke keiki pō lani keia a Kea i hānau,
Keiki ʻakāhi a ka pō, keiki ʻalua a ka pō,
Keiki ʻakolu a ka pō.
ʻO ke kuakoko a ka pō,
E hānau mai auaneʻi ka pō,
ʻO ia hoʻi o ka pō, hānau ka pō,
ʻO ka pō la hoʻi auaneʻi kō luna nei la.

'O wai la hoʻi auaneʻi kō lalo?
'O wai la hoʻi o ka moku?

III

O hānau ka moku a kupu,
A lau, a loa, a aʻa, a muʻo, a liko.
Ka moku ia luna o Hawaiʻi.
'O Hawaiʻi nei nō ka moku.
He pūlewa ka ʻāina, he naka Hawaiʻi,
E lewa wale ana nō i ka lani lewa,
Hanou mai e Wākea, pā hano ia.
Mālie ʻikea ka moku me ka honua,
Paʻa ʻia lewa lani i ka lima ʻākau o Wākea,
Paʻa Hawaiʻi, laʻa Hawaiʻi, ʻikea he moku.

O ka moku la hoʻi kō lalo nei.
'O wai la hoʻi kō luna, ʻowai la?
O ke ao, ʻoia hoʻi hā.

IV

O hānau ke ao, o hiki aʻe.
O ʻohi aʻe ke ao, o hiki aʻe.
O mokupawa ke ao, o hiki aʻe.
O aka ʻula ke ao, o hiki aʻe.
O moakaka ke ao mālaʻe.
'Ōpukupuku ke ao melemele.
O memele ka ʻōpua he laʻi.
O ʻōpua nui, uli ka ʻōpua hiwahiwa,
O hiwahiwa ka ʻōpua laniʻele,

'Ele'ele ka lani huhulu weo,
Lani 'eka'eka hā'ele'ele,
Hākona, hākuma, hākumakuma,
'O ke ao nui mai he'e ua kaia.
E ho'owiliwili ana e hānau,
'O ia ho'i, 'o ke ao, hānau ke ao.

'O ke ao ho'i hā kō luna nei.
'O wai la auane'i kō lalo la?
'O ka mauna, 'oia ho'i.

v

O hānau ka mauna a Kea,
'Ōpu'u a'e ka mauna a Kea.
'O Wākea ke kāne, 'o Papa, 'o Walinu'u ka wahine.
Hānau Ho'ohoku he wahine,
Hānau Hāloa he ali'i,
Hānau ka mauna, he keiki mauna nā Kea.
O ka lili o Wākea, o ka ha'i i ka hala,
O ke kū kukū lā'au 'ana me Kāne,
I ho'oūka ai iloko o Kahiki-kū.
He'e Wākea, kālewa kona 'ōhua.
Kuamū 'ia e Kāne, kuawā 'ia e Kāne.
Ho'i mai Wākea a loko o lani momoe.
Moe Wākea, moe iā Papa.
Hānau ka lā nā Wākea,
He keiki kapu nā Wākea,
'O ka uluna a Wākea nā Kea nō.
'Oia ho'i hā, o ka mauna, hānau ka mauna.

'O ka mauna auane'i kō lalo nei.
'O wai auane'i kō luna la?
'O ka lā, 'oia ho'i hā.

VI

O hānau ka lā a nā'ū,
O nā'ū ka lā o Kupanole.
'O Kupanole ka lā kōhia,
Kōhia ka lā iā Hina.
'O ke kukuna o ka lā pa'a,
'O ka pe'a o Hilinamā, o Hilinehu,
'O ka lālā o ke kamani,
'O ka hui o ke kamani 'ula.
'O ka 'ēheu o Halulu,
Ke ha'ina mai lā, ha'i,
Ke hakia mai la e ka lā,
E ke keiki hele lani ā Kea.
'O Wākea ka i lalo, o ka lā ka i luna,
'O ke keiki ia ā Kea i ho'okauhua ai.
'O ia ho'i o ka lā, hānau ka lā.

'O ka lā auane'i kō luna.
'O wai auane'i kō lalo nei?
'O ka moana, 'oia ho'i hā.

VII

Hānau ka moana ā Kea,
O nā nalu nā Kea, o ke kai nā Kea,
O kai kāne, o kai wahine nā Kea,

O koʻa kū, o koʻa hālelo ulu nā Kea,
O hoʻowiliwili a ka iʻa iloko o ka moana.
Uliuli, ʻeleʻele nei lae o ka moana.
O ka moana auaneʻi kō lalo nei.
ʻO wai auaneʻi kō luna e?
ʻO Kū, ʻo Lono, ʻo Kāne, ʻo Kanaloa,
ʻO Kaʻekaʻe, ʻo Mauli,
O haku o ka pule, o nuʻu pule,
O nuʻu kahuna, o ʻeliʻeli holo i mua kapu,
O ʻeliʻeli holo imua noa, noa ka hānau ʻana o ke aliʻi.

Hānau Kū, ʻo Kū la auaneʻi hoʻi kō luna.
ʻO wai la hoʻi kō lalo nei, ʻo wai la?

ʻO Hāloa, puka kānaka, laha nā aliʻi.
Loaʻa i luna nei ʻo Ka-lani Mehameha,
ʻEkāhi ka lani la, ʻekāhi o luna nei.
ʻO Ka-lani Kau-i-ka-ʻalaneo ʻelua o luna nei.
Pili lāua, ua mau paha, ʻoia paha?
ʻO Ka-lani-nui-kua-liholiho ʻakāhi,
I ke kapu la, ʻakāhi o luna nei.
ʻO Ka-lani ʻo Kau-i-ke-ao-uli, ʻalua o luna nei,
Pili lāua, ua mau paha.

ʻOia e.

❀ ❀ ❀

Birth Chant for Kau-i-ke-ao-uli

I

The chiefess gave birth,
she bore in labor above,
she lay as in a faint, a weakness at the navel.
The afterbirth stirred at the roots, crept in darkness,
in waves of pain came the bitter bile of the child.
This was a month of travail,
of gasping labor,
a writhing to deliver the chief.
He is this chief, born of a chiefess.

Now a chief shall be here above.
Who shall be below?

Born was the earth, rooted the earth.
The root crept forth, rootlets of the earth.
Royal rootlets spread their way through the earth
    to hold firm.
Down too went the taproot, creaking
like the mainpost of a house, and the earth moved.
Cliffs rose upon the earth, the earth lay widespread:
a standing earth, a sitting earth was the earth,
a swaying earth, a solid earth was the earth.
The earth lay below, from below the earth rose.
The earth was Kea's, to Kea belonged the earth.

The earth was Papa's, to Papa belonged the earth,
the earthly firstborn borne by Papa.
He is this earth, the earth that was born.

The earth shall be here below.
Who shall be above?

    II

Born was the night above,
born was the night up here.
The heavens slid away into the night, swift came the
    afterbirth.
The nights came closer together, stretching along
until came a separation, making distinct the night
    of Mahina-leʻa.
The night turned, closeness became separated.
This is the royal offspring of night borne by Kea,
first child of the night, second child of the night,
third child of the night.
The night lay in travail
to give birth to the night.
He is this night, the night newly born.

Who shall be below?
Who shall be upon the island?

    III

Born was the island, it grew, it sprouted,
it flourished, lengthened, rooted deeply, budded,
    formed tender leaves.

That was the island over Hawai'i.
Hawai'i itself was an island.
The land was unstable, Hawai'i quivered,
moved freely about in space,
Wākea recognized the island, Hawai'i recognized
    remained.
Visible were island and earth,
held in heavenly space by the right hand of Wākea,
Hawai'i was held, Hawai'i was seen, an island.

Down here shall be an island.
Who shall be above—Who?
The cloud, that is who it shall be.

     IV
The cloud was born, it rose and appeared.
The cloud thrived, it rose and appeared.
The cloud came at dawn, it rose and appeared.
The cloud flushed with a reddish tinge, it rose and
    appeared.
The cloud rose and appeared in clearest configuration,
    turned yellow and menacing.
The horizon cloud hung yellow over a calm sea.
A swelling cloud, a dark cloud,
a cloud whose deepening darkness turned to black
in a sky already black with feathery clouds of dusk,
a sky heavy with blackness, rough, lowering,
a sky speaking in threat:

a vast cloud foretelling the approach of rain.
The sky writhed in labor to give birth.
He is this cloud: thus it was born.

A cloud shall be up here.
Who shall be below?
The mountain, that is who it shall be.

v

Born of Kea was the mountain,
the mountain of Kea budded forth.
Wākea was the husband, Papa Walinuʻu was the wife.
Born was Hoʻohoku, a daughter,
born was Hāloa, a chief,
born was the mountain, a mountain-son of Kea.
Jealous was Wākea, he revealed his fault,
told of his smiting Kāne with a club
in battle, fought in Kahiki-kū.
Wākea was routed, fled in confusion with his family.
None spoke to Wākea save in whispers, but Kāne
    shouted.
Wākea returned to the sky seeking a wife.
He mated, sleeping beside Papa as mate.
The sun was born to Wākea,
a sacred offshoot of Wākea,
the growth of Wākea was Wākea's own.
He was this mountain's growing, this chief: so was the
    mountain born.

The mountain shall be down here.
Who shall be above?
The sun, that is who shall be above.

VI

The sun was born to be mine,
mine the sun of Kupanole.
At Kupanole the sun held back,
the sun held back for Hina's sake.
Rays of the sun made secure
the boundaries of Hilinamā, of Hilinehu,
joined the branch of a *kamani* tree
to the linked branches of the red *kamani*.
The wings of Halulu were broken, broken.
They were severed by the sun,
by the sky-voyaging sun of Kea.
Wākea was below, above was the sun,
the sun-child born to Kea.
He it was, the sun-child: the sun brought to birth.

The sun shall be above.
Who shall be below?
The ocean, that is who shall be below.

VII

The ocean was born of Kea,
the surf for Kea, the sea for Kea,
the wild sea, the gentle sea for Kea,
the coral beds, coral caverns that grow for Kea,

the fish who twist and turn in the surge.
Deep black were the headlands pointing seaward,
broad lay the ocean spread out below.
Who shall be above?
Kū, Lono, Kāne, Kanaloa,
Kaʻekaʻe and Mauli,
composers of prayers, givers of prayers,
high priests who uttered solemn prayers in sacred
    places,
voiced them in places free: free of kapu was the place
    of the chief!

Born was Kū, let him remain above.
Who shall be below? Who indeed?

From Hāloa men came forth, chiefs multiplied.
Chief Ka-mehameha was conceived above,
the first chief, the first up here.
The Chiefess Kau-i-ka-ʻalaneo was the second up
    here.
They joined, clung together. Was it not so?
Ka-lani-nui-kua-liholiho was the first
to inherit the kapus, the first up here.
Chief Kau-i-ke-ao-uli was the second up here.
Brothers are they, close joined: they hold firm to
    one another.

So it is.

≈≈≈≈≈≈≈

NOTES

I

Kea (for Wākea) and Papa: Progenitors of chiefs. The birth of the prince is linked to cosmic events and these are personified and mythologically defined in the mating of the sky-father, Wākea, and the earth-mother, Papa.

II

Born was the night: Night (*pō*) here refers to the world of the unseen as revealed in dreams. Thus the gestation and birth of the child was accompanied by a series of revelations of increasing intensity, until there appeared Mahina-leʻa, when "the moon shone at its brightest"— probably the act of parturition. The sequence of three "royal offspring borne by Kea" may be an allusion to the three children of Ke-ōpū-o-lani sired by Ka-mehameha.

V

Hoʻohoku and Hāloa: Hoʻohoku was a daughter of Wākea by whom she bore offspring. Hāloa was the name of two sons born of the mating. The first son was the taro plant; the second (an ancestor of Kau-i-ke-ao-uli) was a man. The name Hāloa (literally, 'long breath') is based on the form *hā*, referring to breath expelled to impart *mana*, 'magical power', as when a priest would exclaim "Hā!"

Kāne: A comprehensive source-god worshiped by early Polynesians as the god of life, water, sunlight, and the whole world of nature. Three other major gods are invoked later in the chant. Kanaloa, companion of Kāne, is introduced as a god of healing. Kū, a male fertility symbol, was regarded as a god of human activities, especially canoe-making and war. Lono, also concerned with fertility, presided over the peaceful activities of fishing and agriculture.

VI

sun of Kupanole: The allusion is obscure, but appears to refer to a place involved in legends of the moon-goddess Hina. The "boundaries of Hilinamā, of Hilinehu" likewise may be a reference to mythical events connected with the monthly lunar cycles. Malo, *Hawaiian Antiquities*, lists Hilinamā as the name of a month and Hilinehu as the name of both a month and a star.

Halulu: A mythical bird and messenger of the high gods, one of the sons of the goddess Haumea, mother of Pele and her sisters. The historian Kamakau noted that the feathers that rise and fall on the heads of images in answer to *kahuna* prayers were believed by Hawaiians to come from the sacred birds Halulu and Kuwaʻa—"wonderful feathers made out of particles of water from the dazzling orb of the sun" (Beckwith, *Hawaiian Mythology*, pp. 91–92).

VII

Kaʻekaʻe and Mauli: Two legendary, if not historic, men famous for their religious piety. The gods kept them alive until extreme old age. In a chant honoring Ka-mehameha, *Fallen Is the Chief* (*Haui ka Lani*), they are mentioned as forebears (*kupuna*) of Ka-mehameha.

Kau-i-ka-ʻalaneo: Literally, 'placed in the clear sky'; another name for Queen Ke-ōpū-o-lani, 'the flower opening in the sky'.

Ka-lani-nui-kua-liholiho: Liholiho, Ka-mehameha II (1792–1824), elder son of Ka-mehameha I by Ke-ōpū-o-

lani. After his father's death, the widowed Queen Ka-ʻahu-
manu proclaimed that, according to Ka-mehameha's will,
she and Liholiho would rule over the Kingdom. Both
Liholiho and his sister-wife, Queen Ka-māmalu, died of
measles while in London in 1824, when on a mission to dis-
cuss the possibility of a British alliance with Hawaiʻi.

The Old Way
and the New

THE CHANTS APPEAR to be parts of two separate
compositions, quoted from by Samuel M. Kama-
kau, nineteenth-century historian and politician, in
a tribute to Kau-i-ke-ao-uli, Ka-mehameha III, for
his encouragement of education in Hawai'i and his
capacity for adapting his government to Christian
customs and engrafting foreign political procedures
upon the workings of his monarchy.

Kamakau, himself a zealous convert, writing
during the 1870s for a Hawaiian newspaper, wanted
to show how the Hawaiians' love for their tradi-
tional poetry had helped them, after the abolition of
the eating-kapu in 1819 and the arrival of the first
American missionaries a year later, to channel their
religious energies into new molds of belief, with
different modes of learning and communication.
Kamakau told of how the Christian measures insti-
tuted by Liholiho, Ka-mehameha II ('Io-lani), and
by his newly converted idol-smashing relatives,
Queen Ka-'ahu-manu and the chief Ka-umu-ali'i,
were continued under Liholiho's younger brother,
Kau-i-ke-ao-uli. Indeed, when he was only eleven
years old, the boy-king delivered a royal procla-

mation at Honua-kaha in 1824, promulgating "the government of learning."

Longhouses to serve as schoolrooms seemed to spring up almost overnight, for "if a landlord refused to build he lost his post." In every village, in upland valley as by shore, the people—from children to bearded men—were gathered into the schools. And the Hawaiians, according to their historian, proved to be better than diligent, or merely cheerful, pupils. They were joyous. This was because the "concert exercises by which they were taught"—namely, their group recitations and choral readings and repeatings—"delighted the people." There is no better illustration of the Hawaiians' communal love of eloquent language than Kamakau's own style, however less forceful in translation than in his ancestral tongue:

> The rhythmical sound of the voices in unison as they rose and fell was like that of the breakers at Wai-a-lua or like the beat of the stick *hula* in the time of Pele-io-holani and Ka-lani-'ōpu'u.

> *A ea mai ke kai o Wai-a-lua*
> [Let the sea of Wai-a-lua ascend]

> Because they took so much pleasure in the old chants, they used the old tunes for the recitations in unison.

> *Mai mālama hou i nā akua lā-au*
> [Keep no more wood gods]

That is how the government of learning moved along
quickly so that within half a year there were thousands
of persons who knew how to read, write, and spell.
... "I want a government of learning," said the King,
and the chiefs supported him. The King said, "I give my
Kingdom to God." (*Ruling Chiefs*, pp. 423–424)

❀ ❀ ❀

Ke Kai o Wai-a-lua

A ea mai ke kai o Wai-a-lua,
Wawā nō ʻōlelo ʻokoʻa i pali,
Nūnū me he ihu o ka puaʻa hae la,
ʻAko ka lau o ka nalu piʻi i ka pali.

Ku pali Kai-aka i ka ʻino,
ʻIno ka lae o Kukui-lau-ʻānia,
He Maka-nui.

Makani me he ao la ka leo o ke kai,
Kuli pāʻia wawā ka uka a Lihuʻe,
O me he ʻōkaʻa i ke kula,
Ke kula hahi a ke kai e halulu nei,
Halulu ma ke Koʻolau.

Text: Samuel M. Kamakau, *Ruling Chiefs of Hawaii*,
pp. 423–424. Title assigned.

Hoʻolono ʻEwa,
ʻAʻole i ʻike i ka poʻina a ka nalu,
Kuhihewa wale nō Wahi-a-wā, e.

🌺 🌺 🌺

The Sea of Wai-a-lua

Let the sea of Wai-a-lua ascend,
let the echo carry into the hills
like the grunt of wild boar
while the wave, the climbing surf, uproots seaside
    leaf from cliff.

Kai-aka cliff stands above the storm,
the headland of Kukui-lau-ʻānia faces into the storm
breasting the god of the storm, Maka-nui
    the big wind.

The sea's voice rises, swells on the wind,
deafening the uplands of Lihuʻe.
Borne along field and plain,
thunder of ocean tramples the plain,
    rumbling over Koʻolau.

ʻEwa listens,
unaware of waves breaking, resounding,
mistakes their roar for Wahi-a-wā.

≋≋≋≋≋

NOTES

The sea of Wai-a-lua: Wai-a-lua is the name of a bay, a district, and a village on the northern shore of O'ahu, famous from ancient times for its traditions associated with legendary migrations and the ancestry of ruling chiefs. One old belief is that a certain Nana-kaoka and his wife, representatives of the Ulu line of early migrating families, were the founders on O'ahu of a sacred place in the Wai-a-lua region for the birth of high chiefs. There are numerous references in old Hawaiian poetry to the thunderous waves at Wai-a-lua being carried as far inland as Wahi-a-wā (literally, 'place of noise'). Such passages sometimes refer not merely to the ocean's roar, but may also connote the sound of ceremonial drums signaling the birth of a royal chief.

Ko'olau: Windward mountain range on O'ahu; also term for windward side of various islands.

'Ewa: Name of a district west of Honolulu; commonly used locally today as a geographical direction.

❀ ❀ ❀

Ke 'Li'i o ke Ola Mau

Mai mālama hou i nā akua lā'au,
E huli kākou i ke 'Li'i ola mau,
Maika'i e ho'onui i ke Akua maika'i.

Pēlā mai 'Io-lani kō Hawai'i.

Ua hiki mai nei ke kānāwai mau,
Ke hau'oli nei kō kākou na'au,
Kō 'Io-lani makua Ka-'ahu-manu
    me Ka-umu-ali'i,
E mana'o i ke Akua kō luna Ali'i.

Nā lāua kākou i kauoha mai,
E paulele mau i ke Akua maika'i,
I ola ka 'uhane o kākou a pau:

Ka pūaneane ke ao mālama mau,
A kaua mai nei ka po'e kīmopō,
Ua mālama mai Iesu iā kākou.

Iehova ke Akua kā kākou e hāpai,
I ka pu'uhonua kākou e ola ai.

🌸 🌸 🌸

The Lord of Eternal Life

Keep no more wood gods.
Turn to the Lord of eternal life.
Best exalt the best of gods!

So spake 'Io-lani, Chief of Hawai'i.

Hither have come laws everlasting
bringing joy to uplifted hearts.

'Io-lani's foster-mother, Ka-'ahu-manu, and Ka-
    umu-ali'i
taught us to believe in God, King overhead.

These two have counseled us
to put faith in the good God
that our souls may surely be saved.

Let us dwell in the land of eternal light
so that when enemies come to destroy us
Jesus will give us His care.

Jehovah is the God whose glory we laud,
our refuge for life without end!

A Surfing Song

SURFING IN EARLY Hawai'i served as a way of
life, as it does for some people today. In ancient
times, and on into the nineteenth century, surfing
was a discipline for heroes. "It was the center of a
circle of social and ritual activities," as Ben Finney
tells us, "that began with the very selection of the
tree from which the board was carved, and could end
in the premature death of a chief" (*Surfing*, p. 35).
Both males and females regarded surfboards as
prized pieces of property and selecting their names
required much thought.

Since a chief's status as a leader depended, in
part, on strength, extreme agility, and courage, it
is not surprising that chiefs above all, whose wealth
consisted partly in their leisure time, excelled in the
dangerous arts of surfing, *hōlua* sledding, and canoe
leaping. The relative decline of surfing in the later
nineteenth century (until its revival and commercial-
ized exploitation in more recent times) ran parallel
to the falling away, to the point of dissolution, of
other native traditions, such as those of ancient dance
as represented in the sacred hula.

The chant here presented under the assigned title
A Surfing Song is an adaptation of a fine traditional
chant known as *A Name Chant for Naihe*. Naihe was

an accomplished orator and athlete of Kona, island
of Hawai'i, who flourished during the first thirty
years of the nineteenth century. Though not of royal
rank, he was a son of Keawe-a-heulu, one of the lead-
ing warriors of Ka-mehameha the Great. His wife
was the chiefess Ka-pi'o-lani, a notable Christian
convert, who had given up other husbands for the
sake of Naihe and her religion. Naihe's fellow chiefs
were jealous of his skill as a surfer and conspired to
kill him. They invited him to a surfing contest at
Hilo, and then, as Ben Finney tells the story:

> ... they secretly agreed that no one, once he had paddled
> out to the breakers, could return to the beach until he
> heard his personal chant from the shore.
> The contest had already started when Naihe arrived.
> Although his chanter was with him, Naihe, in his ig-
> norance of the secret pact, let the old woman sleep while
> he paddled out. He was already in water when he learned
> of the rule and was, therefor, marooned off the shore.
> Luckily, a Puna chief decided to aid Naihe and sent a
> servant to wake the old woman. When she learned of her
> master's plight, she rushed to the beach. With tears
> streaming down her withered cheeks, the old woman stood
> on the shore and chanted. ...
> Naihe was thus allowed to return to shore, the plot to
> kill him was foiled. (*Surfing*, pp. 45–46)

The text of the chant here translated bears little
relation to the original chant as performed by
Naihe's faithful old chanter. The present version

is based on a much shortened and somewhat mod-
ernized text as adapted and refurbished by court
chanters of the Ka-lā-kaua period. King Ka-lā-kaua
simply "adopted" *A Name Chant for Naihe* and
added it to his collection to bring luster to his own
dynasty, since he could claim to be a relation of
Naihe's family.

❀ ❀ ❀

He Mele He'e Nalu

Ka nalu nui, a kū ka nalu mai Kona,
Ka malo a ka māhiehie.
Ka 'onaulu loa, a lele ka'u malo.
O kaka'i malo hoaka,
O ka malo kai, malo o ke ali'i.
E kū, e hume a pa'a i ka malo.

E ka'ika'i ka lā i ka papa 'o Halepō
A pae 'o Halepō i ka nalu.
Hō'e'e i ka nalu mai Kahiki,
He nalu Wākea, nalu ho'ohu'a,
Haki 'ōpu'u ka nalu, haki kuapā.

Text: N. B. Emerson, *Unwritten Literature: The Sacred
Songs of the Hula*, pp. 35–36. Title assigned.

Ea mai ka makakai he'e nalu.
Kai he'e kākala o ka moku,
Kai kā o ka nalu nui,
Ka hu'a o ka nalu o Hiki-au.
Kai he'e nalu i ke awakea.

Kū ka puna, ke ko'a i uka.
Ka mākāhā o ka nalu o Kuhihewa.
Ua 'ō ia, nohā ka papa!
Nohā Māui, nauweuwe,
Nauweuwe, nakelekele.
Nakele ka 'ili o ka i he'e kai.
Lalilali 'ole ka 'ili o ke akamai,
Kāhilihili ke kai a ka he'e nalu.

'Ikea ka nalu nui o Puna, o Hilo.

❀ ❀ ❀

A Surfing Song

The big wave, the billow rolling from Kona,
makes a loincloth fit for a champion among chiefs.
Far-reaching roller, my loincloth speeds with the
    waves.
Waves in parade, foam-crested waves of the loin-
    covering sea,
make the *malo* of the man, the high chief.
Stand, gird fast the loincloth!

Let the sun ride on ahead guiding the board named
  Halepō
until Halepō glides on the swell.
Let Halepō mount the surf rolling in from Kahiki,
waves worthy of Wākea's people,
waves that build, break, dash against our shore.

Now sea-spray of surfing looms into sight.
Craggy wave upon wave strikes the island
pounded by a giant surf
lashing spume against a leafy altar, Hiki-au's
  temple.
At high noontime this is the surf to ride!

Beware coral, horned coral on the shoreside.
This channel is treacherous as the harbor
  of Kākuhihewa.
A surfboard smashes on the reef,
Māui splits, trembles, sinks into slime.
Many a surfman's skin is slippery,
but the champion of chiefs skims into shore un-
  drenched
by the feathery flying sea-spray of surfriders.

Now you have seen great surfs at Puna and Hilo!

NOTES

malo: loincloth

Halepō: The significance of the name of Naihe's surfboard is uncertain. However, there is a tradition that Halepō was the name of a surf at Nā-po'opo'o, Kona, which was Naihe's original place of residence. It is quite possible that the athlete's surfboard came to be known by a name associated with his home waters.

Wākea: Name of earliest ancestor of the ruling chiefs in some genealogies. He became the husband of Papa, later of his daughter by her, and thus founded a sacred senior line of descendants.

Hiki-au: Name of the god Lono's *heiau* (temple) at Nā-po'opo'o, Kona, Hawai'i, built by Ka-lani-'ōpu'u, where the Hawaiians draped Captain James Cook with sacred red tapa and fed him consecrated pig. The *heiau* was renovated later by Ka-mehameha I. William Ellis, surgeon with Captain Cook, 1778–1779, made a drawing of Hiki-au, which is reproduced in Kamakau's *Ruling Chiefs*. The name appears to be related to the star called Hiki-'au-moana, 'Hiki which travels by sea'.

harbor of Kākuhihewa: Honolulu harbor, noted in earlier times for its extensive barrier reefs; here referred to as the harbor of a legendary king of O'ahu.

Forest Chant in
Praise of Laka

THE CHANT, A prayer of praise, honors the goddess Laka, tutelary deity and source (*kumu*) of the hula. Laka's forest chant is still occasionally heard in Hawai'i today, as performed by *kumu hula* (hula teachers), and by their pupils, who have been trained in the old tradition.

In earlier times, when the ritual was strictly observed, the chant was recited by a disciple of the goddess, male or female, while gathering grasses, herbs, and other forest greenery to be used as decorative offerings for the altar in the *hālau*, the ceremonial hula hall used for practice and performance. Hawaiians regarded Laka as a member, though not exactly a blood-sister, of the Pele family of fire gods. The chant names Laka as sister and wife of Lono, the high god especially celebrated in the *makahiki* festival, and his mating with Laka represents a union of sky and earth. Besides Laka, other deities of both the female and male pantheon figure in the numerous prayers of the ritual, including the sisters Pele and Hi'i-aka and their mother, Haumea (patron goddess of childbirth, and an earth-mother figure equivalent to Papa), along with all four major Polynesian male deities, Kāne, Kanaloa, Lono, and Kū.

The hula of tradition combined at least three functions, being simultaneously a fertility cult, an organization for practicing various arts of healing and for inculcating cosmetic lore (principles of hygiene and physical beautification), and a school of the combined arts of music, poetry, mime, and dance. The *Forest Chant in Praise of Laka* has helped to keep alive at its very roots an essential element of the ritual magic: the verbal component, as resting especially on the invocation, by name and tribute praise, of the ancient Hawaiian gods.

❀ ❀ ❀

He Kānaenae nō Laka

A ke kuahiwi, a ke kualono,
Kū ana 'o Laka i ka mauna,
Noho ana 'o Laka i ke po'o o ka 'ohu.
'O Laka kumu hula,
Nana i 'a'e ka waokele,
Kāhi, kāhi i mōlia i ka pua'a,
I ke po'o pua'a,
He pua'a hiwa nā Kāne,
He kāne nā Laka,
Nā ka wahine i 'oni a kelakela i ka lani.

Text: N. B. Emerson, *Unwritten Literature: The Sacred Songs of the Hula*, pp. 16–17.

I kupu ke aʻa i ke kumu,
I lau a puka ka muʻo,
Ka liko, ka ʻao i luna,
Kupu ka lālā, hua ma ka hikina,
Kupu ka lāʻau ona a Makaliʻi:

ʻO Mākālei, lāʻau kaulana mai ka Pō mai,
Mai ka Pō mai ka ʻoiāʻiʻo—
I hōʻiʻo i luna, i ʻōʻō i luna.

He luna au e kiʻi mai nei iā ʻoe, e Laka,
E hoʻi ke kōkua pāʻū.
He la ʻūniki nō kāua,
Hāʻikeʻike o ke Akua,
Hōʻike ka mana o ka Wahine,
ʻO Laka, kaikuahine,
Wahine a Lono i ka ʻou-aliʻi.

E Lono, e huʻ ʻia mai ka lani me ka honua!
Nou ʻokoʻa Kūkulu o Kahiki.

Me ke ʻanoʻai aloha, e!
E ola, e!

❀ ❀ ❀

Forest Chant in Praise of Laka

Far off as the ridges of the upland,
behold Laka standing on the mountain,
wreathed in mist, dwelling with the summit cloud.
Laka, goddess and founder of the hula,
rises above the rain forest, presides over
the sacred place, the place where the pig was
    sacrificed
by the pupil priest,
the black boar for offering to Kāne,
Laka's forest companion,
she the foremost woman to mate with gods of the
    sky.

That the root may grow from the source,
that the shoot may put forth and leaf,
the young leaflet push up the unfolding bud,
the branch and fruit thrusting toward the East,
the upward-springing Tree that bewitches fish
during Makali'i's months of summer rains:
Welcome that eternal Tree, Mākālei, revealed by Pō,
Pō's truth-telling Tree,
swelling, ripening, fruiting above!

Now I come to you, Laka, skilled in your art,
for help with girding on the sarong.

This is the rite, the time for showing forth,
you and I with you,
the forest magic of the goddess,
power of Laka, loved sister and wife
of Lono in the clouds.

Lono, join sky with earth!
Yours is the true post, the pillar holding up Kahiki!

For you this greeting, beloved Laka.
Grant us health and life!

NOTES

pig was sacrificed: Emerson, *Unwritten Literature*, says
that the eulogy to Laka "was recited while gathering wood-
land decorations for the altar" (p. 16), but gives no further
details. Neither his translation nor commentary makes the
ritual clear, where and when the "black boar" was slaugh-
tered, nor who exactly performed this important act in the
ceremony. The present translation is based on the ques-
tionable assumption that the "head pupil" or "pupil priest"
of the hula troupe—the *poʻo puaʻa*, as he was called, lit-
erally the 'boar's head'—probably officiated at the sacri-
fice, and that in ancient times the place of the sacrifice
was the forest itself. Elsewhere, in discussing the organiza-
tion of a hula school, Emerson defines the duties of the *poʻo
puaʻa* as including: "the execution of the *kumu*'s judg-
ments and commands," collection of fines, and enforcing
"the penalties imposed by the *kumu*. It fell to him to con-
vey to the altar the presents of garlands, *ʻawa*, and the like
that were contributed to the *hālau*." Perhaps, without stat-

ing so, Emerson was here limiting his remarks to customs
still prevalent in hula schools of the nineteenth century,
when certain of the most primitive practices related both to
Kāne and Laka worship had become vestigial, unrecog-
nizably modified, or had been entirely eliminated.

Makaliʻi: Hawaiian month name, here taken to refer to
the six summer months as a season.

Mākālei: Name of supernatural tree on Molokaʻi, with
a root that was supposed to lure fish into a fish gate or pond.
Haumea, regarded as patroness of childbirth because she
was believed to have introduced natural (in place of
Cesarean) childbirth, used a stick from Mākālei to trans-
form herself from an old woman into a budding girl.
Mākālei is clearly a version of the worldwide Tree-of-
Life symbol.

Pō: Here the realm of the gods and source of revelation as
in dreams or omens. The language of the chant at this point
is characteristic of Polynesian creation myths, in which
the successive stages of creation may sometimes be de-
scribed almost entirely in abstract terms ("From the con-
ception the increase," for example) and sometimes more
concretely, as here where the creative stages are sym-
bolized in the rooting, rising, flowering, and fruiting of
a tree.

the rite: This is given in the Hawaiian text as *ʻuniki,* name
for an initiation ceremony that corresponds to "gradua-
tion" in modern hula schools. Its function was to celebrate,
by honoring the goddess, the proficiency attained by the
disciple in his or her art. Similar rites were practiced in
other ancient arts, such as *lua* (general name for hand-
to-hand fighting). The *Hawaiian Dictionary* notes that the
term *ʻuniki,* is "probably related to *niki,* to tie, as the
knowledge was bound to the student."

Songs from "Pele and Hiʻi-aka"

THE CYCLE OF chants, dance-songs, legends, and prose tales that make up the story of Pele and Hiʻi-aka constitutes the greatest single body of surviving Hawaiian-Polynesian myth in narrative form: "The most outstanding Polynesian journey of song through an archipelago," in the words of Katharine Luomala (*Voices on the Wind*, p. 34).

The cycle opens with an account of the events that lead Pele, together with her numerous sisters and brothers and other kin (the total varies according to the version), to leave her homeland of Kahiki for a long journey ending finally in the Hawaiian Islands. After arriving at the archipelago, the highborn travelers tour from island to island seeking a spot suitable for a homesite, and settle finally on Hawaiʻi, at Moku-ʻāweoweo (land of burning).

While her body lies sunk in trancelike sleep, Pele in spirit form journeys to Hāʻena on the island of Kauaʻi where she meets and falls in love with a young chief, Lohiʻau. He is overpoweringly handsome and an enthusiastic devotee and patron of the hula. When she has spent several days and nights in continuous dalliance in Lohiʻau's arms, Pele returns to her vol-

canic home at Kīlauea crater, and then, reunited in
body and spirit, regains consciousness after her mem-
orable slumber.

Upon awakening, the fire goddess decides to send
one of her sisters to Kaua'i on a mission to fetch
Lohi'au to the volcano, so that she can spend "five
days and five nights" with Lohi'au again as her lover.
Hi'i-aka, Pele's youngest and favorite sister, under-
takes the journey out of loyalty to Pele, who prom-
ises (faithlessly, according to her nature) to protect
Hi'i-aka's precious *lehua* forests in Puna from fiery
depredation.

The main episodes of Hi'i-aka's adventures con-
cern her interisland odyssey, its hardships and dan-
gers, including encounters with water-spirits and
enchanters, and her success at last in reaching Lohi'au
on Kaua'i. The later part of the story tells of the
astonishing reunion of Pele and Lohi'au and its vio-
lent aftermath. The legend achieves dramatic as
well as narrative and lyric power, pathos as well as
beauty and humor, because of the conflict that arises
among the three central characters, for on their
shared journey from Kaua'i to Hawai'i, Hi'i-aka
and Lohi'au have discovered that they are in love.
In the end, Hi'i-aka turns for the first time against
Pele, revolted by her sister's willful and selfish
ways. On the very rim of Kīlauea crater, in full view
of Pele and the assembled family, Hi'i-aka joins
Lohi'au in loving embrace.

In her fury Pele commands the spellbound sisterhood
to destroy Lohiʻau with their fires, but instead the
goddesses are stirred to pity and admiration by
Lohiʻau's beauty. Nor will Pele's own brother-gods
assist her in vengeance. Pele herself finally encircles
the rapt lovers with her flames. Only Lohiʻau is con-
sumed. Her own body being divine, Hiʻi-aka survives
the catastrophe unscathed.

In at least one version of the story, that of N. B.
Emerson, the romance ends as it should, happily. The
wise Hiʻi-aka, true to her indestructible love and her
persevering nature, resolves to dig down through
the volcanic entrails of the earth and recover Lohi-
ʻau's charred remains. After several successful ex-
cavations, beginning with a first stratum where she
vanquishes the god of suicide, Hiʻi-aka reaches the
tenth level. There she is warned by a friend that if
she allows any freshets of water to desecrate Pele's
subterranean chambers, she will be in danger of her
sister's further revenge.

Fortunately, Lohiʻau's spirit and body are even-
tually restored by other means. A Hawaiian *deus
ex machina*, the god Kāne-milo-haʻi, elder brother
of Pele, "broke the stony form into many pieces and
then, by the magical power that was his, out of these
fragments he reconstructed the body of Lohiʻau,
imparting to it its original form and lineaments"
(*Pele and Hiʻiaka*, p. 237).

Though at first listless and somewhat bewildered

by his experiences, Lohi'au recovers his former zest
for life and normal vulnerability to women's love.
After traveling to Honolulu, he attends a *kilu* game
(similar to quoits) in a famous hula hall, just on
the evening when Hi'i-aka is about to join the com-
pany. Though Hi'i-aka, despite her usual prophetic
powers, is at first unaware of Lohi'au's presence (he
had concealed himself behind a neighbor's shoulder
scarf), she precipitates their reunion by singing a
favorite song. The familiar words waken Lohi'au's
memory, for "he had heard them a score of times
before" (p. 238) ...

> Sipping the honeyed fragrance of *lehua*,
> beloved of forest birds ...

and he promptly responds with a song of his own.
He sings of his pain as well as his joy on returning
once again to the crucible of Kīlauea—"love's coun-
try," as he has come to think of it, "beloved Pit of
Kīlauea."

Thus, in this version of the myth, Lohi'au trust-
ingly endows Hi'i-aka, or his image of her, with
the reflection of those same elemental powers of
fire and flame ruled over by her ancient sister. The
difference is that the flames of Hi'i-aka have been
caught, distilled, and transformed into the healing
fragrant flower of love's country, Hi'i-aka's crimson
lehua.

The Coming of Pele

OLD HAWAIIAN CHANTERS and storytellers, when reciting the Pele and Hiʻi-aka legends, would on occasion insert into their narratives a chant in the singing (*oli*) style, a flashback review of Pele's migration from Kahiki with members of her family, with a description of the building of the canoe, the gods who accompanied the party, and incidents of the journey from the homeland.

Various versions of the migration story have been recorded and published. Our version, from Kaʻū, has its own interest. In Kaʻū, as late as the 1890s, among Hawaiians familiar with rites of ancient Pele worship, *The Coming of Pele* was sometimes offered as a morning prayer, performed on the beach after midnight and before dawn, at about two o'clock, to celebrate the beginning of the Hawaiian day.

🌺 🌺 🌺

Ka Huakaʻi a Pele

Mai Kahiki mai ka wahine ʻo Pele,
Mai ka ʻāina o Polapola,
Mai ka pūnohu a Kāne,
Mai ke ao lalapa i ka lani, mai ke ao ʻōpua.

Lapakū i Hawaiʻi ka wahine ʻo Pele.
Kālai i kona waʻa Honua-i-ākea,
Kō waʻa, e Ka-moho-aliʻi, holoa mai ka moku.
Ua ʻoki, ua paʻa ka waʻa o ke akua,
Kō waʻa o Kālai-honua-mea,
Holo mai ke au.

Hele a aʻe aʻe ʻo Pele-honua-mea,
ʻAʻe aʻe kalani ʻai punia mai ka moku.
ʻAʻe aʻe kini o ke ʻkua.

Iā wai ka uli, ka hope o ka waʻa, e nā hoaʻliʻi?
Iā Pele-a-ʻehu, a Menehune.
Ka ʻia ka liu, hoʻonoho ʻia kāu hoe iluna o ka waʻa
ʻO Kū mā lāua ʻo Lono.

Holo ai ka honua ʻāina kau i hoʻolewa moku,
ʻO Hiʻi-aka noʻeau he ʻkua,
Hele aʻe a kōmi i ka hale o Pele.

    Text: Mary Kawena Pukui

E huahua'i i Kahiki, lapa uila e Pele,
E hua'i, e hua'ina ho'i a.

❀ ❀ ❀

The Coming of Pele

From Kahiki came the woman Pele,
from the land of Polapola,
from the rising reddish mist of Kāne,
from clouds blazing in the sky, horizon clouds.

Restless desire for Hawai'i seized the woman Pele.
Ready-carved was the canoe, Honua-i-Ākea,
your own canoe, O Ka-moho-ali'i,
for sailing to distant lands.
Well-lashed and equipped, the canoe of high gods,
your canoe, Sacred-hewer-of-the-land,
stood ready to sail with the ocean current.

Pele-honua-mea embarked, the heavenly one
stepped aboard to sail round Kahiki island.
Multitudes of gods came aboard.

O royal companions, who handled the steering paddle
　　at the stern?

Pele-the-redhead herself was helmswoman, ruler of
    the Menehune.
Kū and Lono bailed out the bilge water,
carried paddles, placed them in station.

Hi'i-aka, the wise sister, next embarked,
boarded the craft to dwell with Pele in her sailing
    quarters,
close to Pele on the long voyage.

Jets of lava gushed from Kahiki.
Pele hurled her lightning,
vomit of flame, outpouring of lava was the woman's
    farewell.

NOTES

Kahiki ... Polapola [Bora Bora] : Kahiki, a variant of
the name Tahiti, here refers to the floating isle from where
the family of Pele emigrated. Both geographical names,
so far as they can be said to point to actual geographical
localities, imply the region of the Society Islands, includ-
ing the Tuamotus.

Ka-moho-ali'i : Pele's eldest brother, known also as king
of the shark-gods.

Sacred-hewer-of-the-land : A name for Pele, alluding to
her powers of cleaving and carving up the landscape.

Pele-the-redhead: This is given earlier in the Hawaiian
text as Pele-honua-mea, literally, 'Pele [of the] reddish
earth'. Some Hawaiians believed that members of the Pele
family were *ʻehu* people, with lighter skin, brown eyes,
and curly brown hair, unlike the darker-skinned Hawaiians.

the Menehune: A legendary race of small people, magical
construction workers, who labored at night building roads,
fishponds, and temples.

Hi'i-aka's Song
at Pana-'ewa

Having promised to bring the handsome chief
Lohi'au of Kaua'i to Pele, Hi'i-aka has set forth on
her journey. Nightfall overtakes Hi'i-aka and her
three young women traveling companions in a dense
forest in the Puna district. The territory is held by an
enchanter and water-spirit who is a cannibal. His scouts,
dispatched earlier, report to him that four human be-
ings, four young women, have entered his forest do-
main. Hi'i-aka, who is a seer gifted with powers of
prophecy, has complete foreknowledge of Pana-'ewa's
evil designs and is in no way disturbed: as the tale runs,
she "kept her own courage at the fine point of seem-
ing indifference; she also inspired her companions
with the same feeling by the calm confidence dis-
played in her singing" (Emerson, *Pele and Hi'iaka*,
p. 32).

❀ ❀ ❀

Kau a Hi'i-aka i Pana-'ewa

Pau ku'u aho i nā kahawai o Hilo,
He lau ka pu'u, he mano ka ihona,
He mano nā kahawai o Kula'i-mano.

He wai o Honoli'i, he pali o Ka-ma'e,
He pali nō Hilo-pali-kū.
I hele 'ia 'o Wai-o-lama o Pana-'ewa,
O Pana-'ewa moku-lehua,
Ku hāo'eo'e ka pili'ula a ka manu.

Ua po'epo'ele Hilo,
Pō Hilo, pō Puna i ka uwahi o ku'u 'āina,
Ola iā kini, ke 'a mai la ke ahi a ka Wahine a—

❀ ❀ ❀

Hi'i-aka's Song at Pana-'ewa

I lose my breath crossing Hilo region's rivers and
    ravines,
countless hills, descents innumerable as I travel
Kula'i-mano's gullies and streams.

Text: Mary Kawena Pukui

There's Honoli'i stream and the cliff called Ka-ma'e,
single cliff among many in spacious Hilo-of-the-
     standing-cliffs.
Wai-o-lama River flows on and on through Pana-'ewa,
Pana-'ewa the rain-drenched forest-island of tallest
     trees,
dense branches of scraggly *lehua,*
'*ōhi'a*'s flame-flower, beloved of forest birds.

Now Hilo darkens. Night falls in Hilo.
Puna, sunk in dusk, glows through my smoky land.
All things stir with life, breathe anew.

The Woman has lighted her fires.

NOTE

lehua, '*ōhi'a*'s flame-flower: *Lehua* is the flower (usually
red) of the '*ōhi'a* tree (*Metrosideros macropus, M. collina*).

Hiʻi-aka's Song at Cape Lani-loa

Hɪʻɪ-ᴀᴋᴀ, ɴᴏᴡ ᴀᴄᴄᴏᴍᴘᴀɴɪᴇᴅ by the girl Wahine-ʻomaʻo (The-woman-in-green), is traveling over-land along windward Oʻahu. Charmed by the scenic landscape, recalling past events and pleasant as-sociations, Hiʻi-aka greets the different headlands, ridges, and capes as if they were loved relatives and old friends.

Lani-loa is a modest peninsula projecting from Lāʻie Point on Oʻahu. At one time it had been guarded by a great water-spirit named Lani-loa, but a certain Kana killed the monster and chopped the body into five tiny islands.

Today the hole where Kana severed Lani-loa's head can easily be seen from the lookout at the end of the promontory. At Lani-loa the sea still constantly washes against the shore of this crumbling land.

❀ ❀ ❀

Kau a Hiʻi-aka i Lani-loa

Lele Lani-loa, ua mālie,
Ke hoe aʻe la ka Moaʻe.
Ahu kai i nā pali,
Kai koʻo lalo, e.
Ua piʻi kai i uka, e.

❀ ❀ ❀

Hiʻi-aka's Song at Cape Lani-loa

Cape Lani-loa flies,
takes a diver's plunge
into a calm sea.
The tradewind breathes.
A rising surf lifts at the foot of cliffs bathed
    in the spray.
The ocean is climbing the hills.

Text: N. B. Emerson, *Pele and Hiʻiaka*, p. 97.

Hi'i-aka's Song
at Wai-a-lua

H I'I-AKA AND WAHINE-'ŌMA'O have passed
through the lands of Lā'ie and Mālaekahana, and
they have rounded the borders of Ka-huku, all in
Ko-'olau-loa district, O'ahu. They cross Wai-mea
Stream by way of a sandbar and climb a rocky bluff,
Kēhu-o-hāpu'u, where they find, in the narrator's
words, "a fine view of the ocean surges, tossing up
their white spray as they ceaselessly beat against
the nearby elevated reef-fringe that parapets this
coast, as well as of the Ka'ala mountains, blue in
the distance" (Emerson, *Pele and Hi'iaka*, p. 98).
Standing on Kēhu-o-hāpu'u, watching the ocean dash
against the bluff below, Hi'i-aka listens to the mas-
sive movement of the waves.

🏵 🏵 🏵

Kau a Hiʻi-aka i Wai-a-lua

ʻO Wai-a-lua, kai leo nui,
Ua lono ka uka o Līhuʻe.
Ke wā la Wahi-a-wā, e.
Kuli wale, kuli wale i ka leo—
He leo nō ke kai, e.

🏵 🏵 🏵

Hiʻi-akaʼs Song at Wai-a-lua

Wai-a-lua, your great-voiced sea
resounds to upland Līhuʻe.
Then it sounds once more at Wahi-a-wā.
Deafened are we by that mighty voice, and stunned—
Oh, the roar of the sea!

Text: N. B. Emerson, *Pele and Hiʻiaka*, p. 99.

Hiʻi-aka's Song
at Ka-ʻena

Hɪʻɪ-ᴀᴋᴀ ᴀɴᴅ Wᴀʜɪɴᴇ-ʻōᴍᴀʻᴏ, having left Wai-a-
lua, continue in the direction of Ka-ʻena, the western-
most point on Oʻahu, said to be named after a relative
of Pele who accompanied her from Kahiki. The
shoreline at Ka-ʻena is laden with legendary mem-
ories. So it is today, and so it was already in Pele's
time, haunted by the past.

Spirits of the dead of Oʻahu leaped from this
general area, once known as Leina-ka-ʻuhane (leap
of the soul), to join their kinsmen in the under-
world. Ka-ʻena provided Māui with a mighty foot-
hold when the trickster demigod cast his giant hook
and line in his unsuccessful attempt to unite Kauaʻi
and Oʻahu, or perhaps all the scattered Hawaiian
islands, into a single island continent. Pele, during
her earlier dream-journey to Kauaʻi, paused at Ka-
ʻena to chide her patriarchal kinsman, the antique
Stone of Kauaʻi, for luring her onward to follow
the music of the hula drums pounding away at
Lohiʻau's bedazzling court at Hāʻena.

🏵 🏵 🏵

Kau a Hi'i-aka i Ka-'ena

Lele ana Ka-'ena me he manu ala,
I ka mālie me he kaha 'ana nā ke ka'upu
Ke one o Nēnē-le'a,
Me he upa'i ala nā ke koa'e
I waho la o ka 'ale o Ka'ie'ie.

Me he kanaka ho'onu'u ala i ka mālie,
Ka papa kea i ke alo o ka 'alā.
Ua ku'i 'ia e ke kai a uli, a nono, a 'ula,
Ka maka o ka 'alā,
E noho ana i ke kai o Kāpeku,
Ka leo o ke kai o ho'oilo ka malama.

Ke kū mai la ka pā'ulu'ā hiwa
Makai ka hō'ailona o ka 'āina.
Ahuwale ka pae ki'i, ka pae newanewa,
Ka pae manu a Kanaloa,
E ho'opaepae ana i ka lae o Ka-lā'au,
Kīhe 'ahe'a ana i ke kai o Ewelua.

Nā 'owae pali o Unulau,
Inu aku i ka wai o Ka-'apu.
Hō'ole ke kupa hūnā i ka wai.
'Ehā ka muliwai wai a Ka-'ena

   Text: Mary Kawena Pukui

ʻEʻena iho la i ka lā o Makaliʻi.
ʻOʻio mai ana i kuʻu maka,
Me he kālana pali ala o Lei-honua.

Honua iho nei loko i ka hikina ʻana mai a nei
　　makani.
Heaha la kaʻu makana i kuʻu hilahila?

O kaʻu wale nō ia o ka leo a.

❀ ❀ ❀

Hiʻi-akaʻs Song at Ka-ʻena

Ka-ʻena reaches out like a bird flying overhead,
a sea-gannet soaring in a still sky
above sandy Nēnē-leʻa,
a boʻsunbird high over the channel of Ka-ʻieʻie—
a flapping of wings.

Like a thirsty man drinking from a pool
so do rocks near Ka-ʻena drink of foamy waves.
Silent pounding has darkened those quiet faces
　　of stone.
Bruised black and red, waterworn,
they have grown ghostly from long attending the
　　sea of Kāpeku,
a wintry seasonʻs song.

Blackened and red from perpetual pounding
stand these sea-wardens of the land:
naked god-forms, unstable god-forms
assumed by Kanaloa who shaped them,
sea-washed bird-forms of the high god
guarding the shore at Cape Ka-lā'au,
sprayed by the sea of Ewelua.

In cliff-steep gullies at Unulau
I too drink of Kā-ʻapu's water.
(The countryman, with surly denial, would hide it
    from strangers.)
Yet at Ka-ʻena four shy streamlets wind seaward
in heat of summer sun.
Their living waters file before me in parade.
Lei-honua's great wall beholds the procession.

With the rising of the wind I am caught by a sudden
    thought.
What shall I, in my shame, give to the four bathers?

My sole gift is a song.

NOTES

Nēnē-leʻa: A stretch of beach at Ka-ʻena Point facing the
Stone of Kauaʻi. The name suggests that sea gulls, resem-
bling the Hawaiian goose (*nēnē*), were common there in
ancient times.

Ka-ʻieʻie: For Ka-ʻieʻie-waho, the channel between Oʻahu and Kauaʻi; literally, 'the outside high [waves]'.

wintry season's song: A melancholy (*kāpeku*) sound, as of blustery gusts of wind characteristic of the rainy or cool season of the year (*hoʻoilo*). The mood of the song contrasts with the sun's blaze and the pervasive calm.

four shy streamlets: Hoʻokala, his informant, told Gilbert McAllister, author of *Archaeology of Oahu*, that "the four hidden waters" Hiʻi-aka discovered at Ka-ʻena and at which she quenched her thirst were named "Ulunui, Koheiki, Ulehulu, and Waiakaaiea." Not much information has survived about the minutely detailed geographical features celebrated in this chant.

Hiʻi-aka's Song for the Stone of Kauaʻi

THE STONE OF Kauaʻi is still visible among other boulders and rocks strewn along Ka-ʻena's ample and otherwise bare shores. A dark ledge outlined by foam, the stone lies offshore and is washed on all sides by the sea. Before centuries of erosion wore it away, the Stone of Kauaʻi perhaps boasted a more arresting and phallic profile than the unimpressive prone slab it is today.

The narrator in *Pele and Hiʻiaka* speaks of rocks at Ka-ʻena seeming to "glow and vibrate as if they were about to melt under the heat of the sun" (Emerson, p. 103). The optical image of quivering heat, still to be encountered sometimes at Ka-ʻena, must have been a familiar experience to the Hawaiian foot-travelers who trudged those coastal trails a thousand years ago.

🌺 🌺 🌺

Kau a Hiʻi-aka nō ka Pōhaku-o-Kauaʻi

Liʻua ke kaha o Ka-ʻena, wela i ka lā.
ʻĀina iho la ka pōhaku a moʻa wela,
Kāhuli ʻoniʻo, holo ana i ka mālie.

Haʻahaʻa ka puka one, kiʻekiʻe ke koʻa,
I ka hāpai ʻia e ka makani, ka Mālua,
Oʻu hoa ia i ke Koʻolau, e.
A pā Koʻolau, hoʻolale kula hulu.

Kāhea ke keiki i ka waʻa,
ʻE holo, oi mālie ke kaha o Nēnē-leʻa.
ʻAʻohe hālāwai me ka ʻino i ka makani,
Ka pīpī lua o ka ʻale i ka ihu o ka waʻa.

He waʻawaʻa ka makani, he naʻaupō,
Ke kai kuʻikē, kōkē nalo ka pōhaku!

Ke kupa hoʻolono kai, ʻo Pōhaku-o-Kauaʻi, e,
A noho ana ʻo Pōhaku o Kauaʻi i kai, e!

Text: N. B. Emerson, *Pele and Hiʻiaka*, pp. 103–104.

⚜ ⚜ ⚜

Hi'i-aka's Song for the Stone of Kaua'i

Ka-'ena's brine-parched shore bakes in the sun.
Streaked with flame, consumed, the great rock
      transformed
sails into stillness, the sea's calm.

Sand holes sink underfoot. Coral heads twist upward
quickened into life by the traveler wind Mālua,
sea-borne companion of mine from Ko'olau.
When Ko'olau blows inland shaggy plains bristle.

"Speed!" shouts the sailor to his canoe.
"Speed on, while Nēnē-le'a's sands lie still.
Here's no beating against storm-blast,
only Mālua's light sea-slap along the bow."

O foolish sailor-boy, forgetting how hungry waves
      devour
staunchest rocks!

Stone of Kaua'i, you've manned this watch for ages.
Hold firm, kinsman mine.
Endure, old settler!

~~~~~~~~~~~~~~~~

NOTE

Mālua: General name for a brisk sea breeze; here perhaps
an allusion to Mālua-hele (literally, 'traveling Mālua'), a

familiar wind on Kauaʻi. Thus Hiʻi-aka is acknowledging Mālua's help in accompanying her to Kauaʻi while at the same time she cautions herself to be patient and strong like the Stone of Kauaʻi. Even the best of winds is variable, storms are still possible.

Lei Chant for Queen Emma

Today one thinks of a lei primarily as something to be worn, usually round the neck or as a wreath on the head, and almost always as made of flowers, though there is nothing wrong with leis made of leaves, shells, ivory, rickrack braid, or even paper, when they are skillfully fashioned to serve as a charming symbol of affection. In old Hawai'i a lei could also be made of words, as well as flowers or seeds or feathers. It could be the gift of "a special song presenting a lei," as in this ceremonial lei chant in praise of Queen Emma.

The historic occasion of the chant here translated is unknown. Queen Emma visited Hilo frequently during her lifetime, and on numerous occasions she was the recipient of all sorts of lei-gifts and offerings.

The ceremony in which this lei chant was given, so far as it can be reconstructed from the chant, took place in Hilo, probably in town, and hence the names of the assembled lei-givers, identified by their home villages, districts, and landmarks. The ceremony has obvious resemblances to the custom of *ho'okupo*: the presentation of gifts to a chief, as a tribute and expression of respect; the usual gifts were fruit, fowl, pigs, tapa cloth, bowls, mainly products of the land, but included gear and valuables of many kinds. A significant feature of the ceremony is that the Queen received the leis and placed them round her neck. It would have been a violation of her sacred rank for persons of lesser rank to raise their hands above her head.

Emma Rooke (1838–1885), who became Queen Emma by her marriage in 1856 to Alexander Liholiho, Ka-mehameha IV, was a granddaughter of John Young, an English mariner, who was one of the two first-known foreigners to settle in the Sandwich Islands. On her mother's side, she was descended from a younger brother of Ka-mehameha I. She owed her foreign-style education primarily to the care of her adoptive father, Dr. Thomas C. Byde Rooke, and to the instruction of American missionary teachers, with supplementary lessons in English history, literature, and French supplied by a genteel English governess.

Though she was an ardent Anglophile, one of the founders of the Episcopal Church in Hawai'i, and steeped in Victorian ideas of what constitutes refinement, she was also lively and warm-hearted and very proud of her Hawaiian ancestry. She was well versed in the traditional lore of her people. Wisely, she wanted all Hawaiians and their friends to "become acquainted with ancient songs, their origin, object, composers, effects—also the history of different events and ceremonies—why one should be and others not—for that is the way our Island history has been preserved—entirely oral." (Queen Emma in a letter to her "Dearest Coz," Peter Young Kaeo, a leper of Moloka'i, 1873, Queen Emma Collection, Archives of Hawaii).

The lei baskets mentioned in the chant were usually made of ti leaves, folded so as to enclose the leis (or lei-making materials) and keep them cool and fresh. Lei pegs, as used in Emma's time, may have simply been a modern adaptation of the Western hatrack, a homemade affair in the form of a wooden slat with pegs. Lei-sellers sometimes use such racks in their stalls today.

❀ ❀ ❀

Lei nō Emalani

E hea aku nō au iā Kalani.
E ō mai 'oe i kō inoa lei!

He kākua nō ka lei i Mō-kau-lele,
He pewa nō ka lei o 'Ohi'a-ka-lani,
He kīhene lei o Kani-'ahiku.

Text: Mary Kawena Pukui

He ʻahiku ka nani o Puna me Hilo
He kilohana lei o Wai-ākea.

Lawea ka lei a kau i Ka-Maka-o-Kū,
Kū mai o kalani Kau-maka,
Ke aliʻi nona ka lei.

O pāpahi i ka lei i ke poʻo,
O hoʻonuʻanuʻa ka lei i ka ʻāʻī.

Ke kui lei ʻo Kolo-pulepule,
He amo lei ʻo Wai-luku.

O ke ola e—

O kahua o ka lei ʻo Wai-ānuenue,
O ka heʻe o ka lei ka iā Wai-loa,
O ka hoʻonoho o ka lei ka iā Wai-ākea,
O ka wili o ka maile ka iā Hina,
O ka paʻa o ka ʻomou ka iā Māui.

Nīnau mai ʻo Kekele-a-Iku:
ʻO wai ke aliʻi nona ka lei?
ʻO wai hoʻi kāu o kalani ka manomano,
O ke aliʻi nona ka lei?

He lei nō Emalani.

❀ ❀ ❀

Lei Chant for Queen Emma

I chant this song in praise of my Queen.
Answer, beloved Queen, to your lei chant!

The lei-carrier comes from Mō-kau-lele,
the bundle-bearer from ʻŌhiʻa-ka-lani,
the lady with the lei-basket from Kani-ʻahiku.

Puna and Hilo are made seven times more beautiful
when bedecked with the finest leis of Wai-ākea.

Bring these leis and present them to
The-Eye-of-Kū, Queen Kau-maka
who now stands forth
in radiance.

She whose leis these are takes them
to crown her head, fall from her neck
her shoulders.

Kolo-pulepule strung them for her,
Wai-luku bore them to her.

May the Queen long so live!

Wai-ānuenue is keeper,
Wai-loa is bestower,
Wai-ākea is arranger,
winder of the *maile* strands is Hina,
the bundle-bearer holding the lei pegs is Māui.

Kekele-a-Iku asks:
Who is the Chiefess these leis are to praise?
What brought so many givers of garlands here
all to foregather in praise?

None but the Queen most worthy of honor.

A lei chant for Emalani.

NOTES

Mō-kau-lele: A forested wilderness inland from Hilo.

'Ōhi'a-ka-lani: Another grove inland from Hilo in the
Puna direction. Bulldozing has destroyed many such fa-
miliar landmarks in recent times.

Kani-'ahiku: Land division in Puna district; literally,
'seven sounds'.

Wai-ākea: A river in Hilo district from which adjacent
land takes its name; also the name of the village de-
stroyed by tidal wave in 1960.

Queen Kau-maka: Honorific name for Emma, literally,
'the object of one's admiration'. The preceding name in
the chant, The-Eye(s)-of-Kū, Ka-Maka-o-Kū, links her
with the god Kū. The allusion to the forest god associated
with trees and wild vegetation is in keeping with the chant.

Kolo-pulepule: A branch of Wai-luku stream, Hilo district.

Wai-luku: Stream and land division, Hilo district.

Wai-ānuenue: Old name for Rainbow Falls, near Hilo;
literally, 'rainbow [seen in] water'.

Wai-loa: Stream and land division, Hilo district; literally,
'long water'.

maile strands: Lei woven of a fragrant twining shrub (*Alyxia
olivaeformis*), member of the periwinkle family. Laka,
the hula goddess, was goddess of the *maile*, one of five
native plants especially used on her altar.

Kekele-a-Iku: Name of a legendary hero; here perhaps
a complimentary reference to some prominent person ob-
serving the ceremony.

Song of the Workers
on Howland Island

L EI-SONGS AS GIFTS of affection can take many forms and need not always involve the giving of flowers. This song, known in Hawaiian as *Pua-ka-'ilima*, has an interesting story behind it. It takes its name from the *'ilima* flower, which also came to be the Hawaiian name of the "pancake" islet about one thousand miles southwest of Hawai'i known to navigators and listed in gazetteers as Howland Island. About 1856–1857, early in the reign of Kamehameha IV and Queen Emma, many Hawaiian laborers were taken to Howland, Baker, Johnston, and other tiny outlying islands of Micronesia to dig guano for sea captains and traders operating out of Honolulu. This chant, dedicated to Queen Emma, was composed by one or several poet-workers among the guano-digging crews.

❀ ❀ ❀

Mele a nā Paʻahana i Pua-ka-ʻilima

Aia e ka nani i Pua-ka-ʻilima,
Kēlā ʻailana noho i ke kai,

Nō kai ka makani la a he Kona,
Haʻihaʻi lau lāʻau o ka uka.

Nō uka ka ʻiwa i kīani mai,
Ke hea mai nei i ka nui kino.

E naue aʻe au me kuʻu hoa,
Me kuʻu komo kaimana i ka laʻi.

Haʻina ka puana nō kuʻu lani,
Nō Emalani nō la he inoa.

Text: Mary Kawena Pukui. Title assigned.

🌺 🌺 🌺

Song of the Workers on Howland Island

There's beauty here on Pua-ka-ʻilima,
island-flower of the western sea

but the Kona wind blowing inland
strips every leaf and tree.

Along the ridge a sea eagle soars
calling, "Come, come back to Hawaiʻi and me."

Now let me walk with my love,
in quiet contentment, alone with my diamond ring.

I go to her soon.

Here's a song for my Queen.
Emalani is her name.

NOTE

Pua-ka-ʻilima: Literally, ' *ʻilima* flower'. The *ʻilima* is
a native shrub of variable size (*Sida*, especially *S. fallax*)
whose flowers have always been popular for use in leis.
They are found in a variety of hues, including yellow,
orange, greenish, and rusty red, and it is said that five hun-
dred flowers are needed to make a single lei.

Errand

THE CHANT COMMEMORATES an errand of mercy in which Ka-mehameha V brought the necessities of life, including native medicines as well as food, to workers on his royal ranch at Hālawa, island of Molokaʻi, during a period when the ranch had exhausted its supplies. Lot Ka-mehameha (1830–1872), King Ka-mehameha V, ruled over Hawaiʻi from 1863 to 1872. He was the last of the Ka-mehameha kings directly descended from the Conqueror.

❀ ❀ ❀

Ka Huakaʻi

Ia aloha ia *Kilauea,*
Lio kākele a o ka moana,
Holo mamua holo mahope.

Kau pono ka ihu i ka makani,
Haki nuʻa ka uwahi i ke kai,
Nome aʻe ka huila malalo,
Hala e ka lae o Ka-lāʻau,

Text: Mary Kawena Pukui. Title assigned.

ʻOni ana Molokaʻi mamua,
Huli aʻe e eke alo i Lā-hainā,
He ukana ka *Kilauea,*
Lū aʻe la i Pā-lāʻau,
Hoʻokahi pahuna malalo.

Kohu ʻāuna manu i ke one,
Ka hoholo i ke ālialia.
E ʻole o Ka-lani Mehameha
Ola ai nei pūʻā hipa,
Nā hipa a Ka-maʻi-puʻu-paʻa.

ʻAi ana i ka lau ʻoliwa.

Haʻina ʻia mai ka puana,
Nō Ka-lani Mehameha he inoa.

❀ ❀ ❀

Errand

Kilauea, beloved ship, sea-roving steed
roams this ocean full-steam ahead
backing and hauling, then the voyage home.

Now *Kilauea*'s prow heads into the wind,
smoke breaks from stack, ripples over the sea,
paddle wheel slowly revolves,
passes Ka-lāʻau Point, Molokaʻi up ahead,

Lā-hainā yonder awaiting freight,
and stops at Pā-lā'au to unload cargo,
heave-ho and shove down below.

Like a flock of seabirds upon a waste of sand
a hungry horde races along this salt-encrusted shore.
Were it not for Chief Ka-mehameha
these creatures would be bereft of all supply,
would be as sheep without forage, no shepherd
were it not for life-bringing Ka-ma'i-pu'u-pa'a the
    Kahuna,
wise in matters of sickness, life and death.

Now let his famished flock feed on olive leaves
given with a King's love.

This is the end of my song
in praise of Chief Ka-mehameha.

NOTES

Kilauea: Government-owned interisland steamer, which
sailed during the 1860s and 1870s.

Ka-ma'i-pu'u-pa'a: A female *kahuna*, expert in native medi-
cine and in prophecy, and a member of the king's house-
hold, commonly reputed to be his mistress.

olive leaves: The Christian symbol of peace and token
of trouble relieved, as in the biblical account of the dove
returning with olive leaves to Noah in the ark.

Mr. Thurston's Water-Drinking Brigade

THE CHANT CELEBRATES an excursion, of unknown date but probably on a Sunday, when members of a rural temperance union hiked from their upland homes on the island of Hawai'i down through the Puna district to the sea. Late in the day they either attended a sermon (to hear the "good news") delivered by the Reverend Titus Coan, or perhaps merely learned that the famous preacher would soon be visiting their neighborhood.

❀ ❀ ❀

Ka Pū'ali Inu Wai a Mī Kakina

He mele Pū'ali Inu Wai
Nō nā keiki a Mī Kakina.
Hao mākou a mālo 'elo'e.

Text: Mary Kawena Pukui

La'i ka nohona o Kahua-iki,
A hiki wale aku i Pānau,
Nānā i ka la'i o Pali-uli,
Kāwaha nā pali o Pūlama,
'Au'au i ka wai o Puna-lu'u,
Hele aku mākou i ke kula loa,
A wela i ka lā o Kaunaloa.
Huli aku nānā iā Kala-pana,
Alo ana Kai-mū i ka 'iu'iu.

'Iu'iu mākou i ka lohe 'ana
I ka nū hou mākai nei:
Aloha nui 'oe e Mī Koana,
Ka makua ha'i ola o ka lāhui!

Ke huli ho'i nei nā keiki
I ka uka 'iu'iu o Lehua.

Ha'ina 'ia mai ana ka puana
Nō ka hui Pū'ali Inu Wai.

❀ ❀ ❀

Mr. Thurston's Water-Drinking Brigade

Here's a song of the Water-Drinking Brigade,
brave warriors of Mr. Thurston's army.
Upstanding lads, girded well we journey forth
sparing no labor though weariness overtake.

Most welcome is our rest amid Kahua-iki's quiet
  countryside.
Next we head for Pānau, cast eyes on peaceful Pali-
  uli,
gaze upward to Pūlama's old wrinkled cliffs,
bathe in Puna-lu'u's stream,
then trudge the long, long road
through sweltering heat of Kaunaloa.
Here we turn aside to view Kala-pana,
with a glimpse of far-off Kai-mū.

Only late in the day do we hear the news,
golden news from the lowland:
Loud greetings to you, Mr. Coan,
preacher of the Word, salvation for the people!

Homeward now we march to our loved ones
in the distant upland of Lehua.

This is our song in honor
of Mr. Thurston's Water-Drinking Brigade!

NOTES

Mr. Thurston: The Reverend Asa Thurston (1787–1868),
native of Massachusetts and organizer of the temperance
union, arrived at Kai-lua, Hawai'i, in 1820 as a member
of the first company of missionaries sent to the Sandwich
Islands by the American Board of Commissioners for For-
eign Missions.

girded well: The temperance union was called Pūʻali Inu
Wai, literally 'water-drinking army'; from *pūʻali*, 'war-
rior', referring to the way Hawaiian fighters tied (*pūʻali*)
their loincloths at the waist so that there would be no
flap dangling for the enemy to seize. "Girded well" is an
allusion to this practice.

Kahua-iki ... Pānau ... Pali-uli ... Puna-luʻu ... Kauna-
loa: Villages or land divisions in the Puna-Kaʻū region.

Kala-pana: Shoreside village famous for its black sands.

Kai-mū: Land division in Puna; literally, 'gathering at
sea', in reference to the crowds that gathered on the shore
to watch surfriders.

Mr. Coan: The Reverend Titus M. Coan (1801–1882), a
native of Connecticut, arrived in 1835 with the seventh com-
pany of missionaries. During the great religious revival of
1838 his powerful sermons won many converts, whom he
baptized by the hundreds at a single preaching. Though
the missionaries Coan and Thurston lived at opposite ends
of the island, their evangelical labors took them regularly,
on foot or horseback, into the hinterland and to all villages
of Hawaiʻi.

Alas for Eve

HYMN-COMPOSING as well as hymn-singing was a common practice in early Hawaiian Sunday schools. Members of sabbath classes, often meeting jointly, would each present a hymn of his own composition. Similar customs of composing and improvising, especially on non-Christian topics, were a popular form of entertainment among Hawaiian women when, perhaps at a "sewing bee," they would vie with one another in displaying cleverness at word-play, throwing out and catching allusions, and so forth.

❀ ❀ ❀

Auwē o ʻEwa

I

Hoʻonoho ʻia ma Edena,
Kīhāpai nani, maikaʻi.
Malimali mai kahi nahesa
Iā ʻEwa make palupalu.

Text: Mary Kawena Pukui

HUI
Auwē o 'eha koni e,
'O Akamu me 'Ewa,
Kō kākou mau kūpuna,
I puni i kahi nahesa.

II
Kāhea mai ke Akua,
"Auhea 'oe, e Akamu?"
'I aku 'oia, "Ua lohe au
A maka'u i kō leo."

III
Auwē ke au iā Noa,
I ke kai nui a Kahinali'i,
Pau pulu 'a'ohe lau kanu
Koe 'o Noa me ka 'ohana.

IV
Auwē ke au iā Mose,
Hoa 'ōlelo o ke Akua.
Pau 'o Pala'o me nā koa
I ka luku 'ia e ke Kai-'la!

🏵 🏵 🏵

Alas for Eve

I

They were placed in Eden,
A garden beautiful and good.
There a serpent beguiled
Gentle-faced Eve.

CHORUS

Alas, a bitter pain came
To Adam and Eve,
Our first parents
Seduced by a serpent.

II

God summoned his child:
"Adam, where are you?"
Adam answered: "I hear you
And am afraid of your voice."

III

Alas, for the time of Noah,
When a great flood came.
All drowned, none survived
Save Noah and his family.

IV

Oh, for the time of Moses,
He who talked with God,
When Pharaoh and his soldiers vanished
By the Red Sea destroyed!

NOTE

IV

the Red Sea: The correct form of ke Kai-'la in the Ha-
waiian text is ke Kai-'ula. The Hawaiian text drops a vowel
for rhythm in chanting.

The Prince's Words
to the Princess

THE PRINCE IS William Charles Luna-lilo (1835–
1874), a grandson of a half brother of Ka-mehameha
I. Luna-lilo ruled briefly as king during the early
1870s. The princess is Victoria Ka-māmalu (1838–
1866), a granddaughter of Ka-mehameha I and
sister of Ka-mehameha IV and his brother, Lot Ka-
mehameha. The chant, in the form of a lover's "com-
plaint" (in the Shakespearean sense of the word),
dramatizes a meeting between Luna-lilo and Victoria
Ka-māmalu in upper Nuʻu-anu Valley, Honolulu,
in which the prince bitterly reproaches the girl for
her rejection of his love. The time of this possibly
historic scene was perhaps 1855 or 1856.

Oral tradition has attributed the authorship of
the chant to Luna-lilo himself. Some Hawaiians to-
day believe that the author may have been David
Ka-lā-kaua, but the evidence upon which this claim
is based has not been explained. The tradition of
Luna-lilo's authorship is plausible on various bio-
graphical grounds, if not easily provable today. Lady
Franklin, the much-traveled widow of the Arctic ex-
plorer Sir John Franklin, in her unpublished diary
written in Hawaiʻi in 1861, jotted down certain

details about the young prince. Her information
consisted largely of current gossip about Luna-lilo's
character and conduct, much of which seems in close
accord with the character and situation of the persona
revealed in the chant. Lady Franklin's notations
on "Prince William Lunalilo, the King's first cousin,
being the son of Kanaina and Kekauluohi, sister of
Kinau, the King's mother," run as follows:

> After the present heir apparent, Prince Lot Kameha-
> meha and Princess Victoria, he would be the rightful
> claimant to the Throne. He is a young man of about 24
> yrs of age of remarkable talent, good-looking, well-read
> and of very gentlemanlike manners, understanding and
> speaking English better even than his own language,
> but with all this hopelessly given to drink, and lost to all
> the promise of his earlier years. Mr. Pease thinks this
> is partly owing to the restraint under which he was held
> by the Missionaries who had charge of his education
> and with whom Mr. P. used to remonstrate about their
> keeping him without money, for want of which he would
> borrow and even steal. Mr. Pease has often given him a
> few dollars. He was betrothed to the Princess Victoria
> in their childhood, but when at an early age they wished
> to be married, it was opposed by the King, who is sup-
> posed to have been afraid of his talents and of his large
> estates and influence in Hawaii, which being a conquered
> island is not too loyal in its disposition.
>
> After this disappointment, the young Prince took to
> drinking and the Princess refused David Kalakaua, who
> proposed to her. More recently, the King gave acqui-
> escence to the marriage of his sister with L[unalilo], the
> Princess still desiring it, and all the preparations were

made, Mr. Armstrong being engaged to marry them,
when L. came and said he did not mean to marry Victoria
and should get into such a state of drunkenness for the
occasion as would make it impossible for the marriage
ceremony to take place.

Thus the marriage [was] finally broken off. The
misconduct of the Princess with Mr. Monsarrat may
have been the cause of the Prince's objection to the lady
on the 2d occasion and of the King's wish for the mar-
riage. The Prince it is said is irrecoverably ruined—he
knows he is acting so as to lead him rapidly to the grave
but he professes to be perfectly indifferent to this.

The young Prince was a great admirer of Shakespeare,
and used when in a state of undue excitement to go about
the city on horseback, gathering the people about him
at the corners of streets and reciting passages from his
plays, or sometimes a dispatch of Mr. Wyllie's, [Minister
of Foreign Relations] addressed to the Minister of the
French or some other [unfinished] (Korn, *Victorian
Visitors*, pp. 305–306)

Though not an exact word-for-word translation,
the rendering of the chant here into English is never-
theless an attempt to convey faithfully the "hid-
den story" implicit in its structure, particularly in
its pattern of three very traditional metaphorical
images: the symbolism of the upland pool, the
tempest in the harbor and lowland, and the return
in the end to the forest with its birds and flowers.

Though traditional in imagery, the poem pos-
sesses even in the original Hawaiian some of the
qualities of the dramatic monologue as developed

by nineteenth-century English poets, including
Byron, Tennyson, and Browning, whose widely
anthologized poems in the monologue form may
well have been familiar to Luna-lilo. A central fea-
ture of such poems is the mode of presentation, in
which, as in the chant, we are given only the words
of the embittered lover, never the presumed replies
or the interjections of the sorrow-stricken—or sullen?
—lady.

❀ ❀ ❀

Ka ʻŌlelo a ke Aliʻi Kāne i ke Aliʻi Wahine

ʻAʻole i manaʻo ʻia
Kāhi wai aʻo ʻAle-koki.
Hoʻokohu ka ua i uka,
Noho mai la i Nuʻu-anu.

Anuanu makehewa au
Ke kali ana i laila.
Kainō paha ua paʻa
Kou manaʻo i ʻaneʻi.

Text: Emerson, *Unwritten Literature: The Sacred Songs
of the Hula*, pp. 108–109. Title assigned.

Āu i hoʻomalu ai
Hoʻomalu ʻoe a malu,
Ua malu neia kino
Mamuli o kō Leo.

Kau nui aku ka manaʻo,
Kāhi wai aʻo Kapena.
Pani ā paʻa ʻia mai
Nā māno wai aʻo uka.

Ahu wale nā kiʻo wai
Nā papahele o luna.
Maluna aʻe nō wau
Ma ke kūʻono liʻiliʻi.

Ma waho aʻo Māmala,
Hao mai ana ehuehu,
Pulu au i ka huna-kai
Kai heʻeheʻe i ka ʻili.

Hoʻokahi nō koa nui,
Nāna e ʻalo ia ʻino.
ʻInoʻino mai nei luna
I ka hao a ka makani.

He makani ʻāhaʻi lono,
Lohe ka luna i Pelekane.
A ʻoia pouli nui,
Mea ʻole i kuʻu manaʻo.

I 'ō i 'ane'i au,
Ka pi'ina la a'o Ma'ema'e,
E kilohi au i ka nani
Nā pua i Mauna-'ala.

He 'ala onaona kou,
Ke pili mai i 'ane'i,
O a'u lehua 'ula i luna,
'Ai 'oho a nā manu.

The Prince's Words to the Princess

I've no interest in the Pool of 'Ale-koki.
I scorn people who live in flatlands.
Here where cold rains haunt Nu'u-anu's slopes
I weep and wait and freeze—waiting for nothing.

I loved you once, I believed you.
Even I thought you were true.
You made me swear to be loyal and remember.
Remember your own oath and keep it true.

For this body, beloved, brims with my love.
At the thought of your mouth my heart leaps
with love remembered in a magic pool.
At brink of Ka-pena Pool no magic now
in this cool watershed of upland Nu'u-anu.

You tell me it is fenced, cut off, kapu.
Oh yes, the water-heads are tightly sealed.
Why hide your fountains, dear?
Let descending skies pour down their lesson.

Perhaps you keep me lodged here hung up in the
     cleft
of a dainty rock because teasing amuses you.
Perhaps more than you know, or even I fear perhaps,
I am a man already lost and sinking, in a gulf of
     sorrow.

As a wild wind hurls itself against an unyielding surf
I too am hurled naked against Māmala's spume.
But when did sailor-warrior of old question his in-
     sistent heart
if committed by it to outface the furious brine?

Dark clouds scale a tempestuous sky.
Driven by gossiping winds this tale of ours
reaches lofty ears at Beretania.
Though tale-bearing winds gossip afar
nought care I for darkest storm.
Much less for royal listener!

Now as we climb a winding way at Ma'ema'e,
here where buds of Mauna-'ala shed the fragrance
we knew from childhood only too well,
what flower will burn from your body
if I, beloved, lie in your arms?

When will mine, Pele's scarlet *lehua,*
breathe again for you such sweetness as forest birds
seek in fire of sunlight, fire of darkness,
before tiring into sleep?

~~~~~~

NOTES

'Ale-koki: N. B. Emerson, who published a text of the
song in his *Unwritten Literature of Hawaii,* supplies useful
interpretation: " 'Ale-koki . . . , a name applied to a por-
tion of the Nu'uanu stream lower down than the basin and
falls of Kapena . . . , symbolizes a flame that may once
have warmed the singer's imagination, but which he dis-
cards in favor of his new love, the pool of Kapena. The
rain, which prefers to linger in the upland . . . , typifies
his brooding affection. The cold, the storm, and the tem-
pest that rage at Māmala . . . —a name given to the ocean
just outside Honolulu harbor—and that fill the heavens
with driving scud . . . represent the violent opposition in
high quarters to the love match. The tale-bearing wind,
makani-āha'i-lono . . . , refers no doubt, to the storm of
scandal. The use of the place names Ma'ema'e and Mauna-
'ala seems to indicate Nu'uanu as the residence of the
Princess."

Beretania: This is given in the Hawaiian text as Pelekane,
Hawaiianized form of "Britain." In early days the Ha-
waiians sometimes referred to the palace grounds in
Honolulu and their general vicinity as Pelekane. The al-
lusion here, of course, is to King Ka-mehameha IV himself.

Ma'ema'e: A hilly slope in Nu'u-anu Valley; literally, 'clean, pure, attractive'.

Mauna-'ala: Literally, 'fragrant mountain'; the setting since 1863 of the Royal Mausoleum.

Forest Trees of the Sea

THE DATE OF the song is believed to be the early 1860s. Though the whaling industry was well on the wane in the 1850s, the old sailing ships with their towering masts continued to be seen in Honolulu harbor through the 1880s.

❁ ❁ ❁

Ka Ulu Lā'au o Kai

E 'ike auane'i 'oe
I ka ulu lā'au o kai,
Kai aloha na'u o Māmala,
Kai a'oa'o me ke aloha.

O ka home a'e o Lē'ahi,
Oni ana Pu'u-loa i ke kai,
Loa ke ki'ina a ke aloha.

E kau paha i ka palapala,
Polo'ai aku iāia,
E waiho aku a ho'i mai,
E maliu mai 'oe e ka hoa.
A hiki mai 'oe, pono au.

Text: Mary Kawena Pukui

Haʻina ʻia mai ka puana
I ka ulu lāʻau ma kai.

❀ ❀ ❀

Forest Trees of the Sea

No, it is not too soon.

I have seen in my heart
that sea of forest trees
of tall-masted ships returning
to Honolulu's harbor of Māmala,
making every sea-murmur a word—
Māmala's murmur of unresting love.

Love's home is Diamond Head.
Love's shelter is where Pearl Harbor hills reach out
    to sea.
Love's gaze is keen and long.

Perhaps I should write a letter.
Perhaps I should show my love by asking his:
Come back, dear love, bring ease to me,
comfort of mind.

For you I sing my song
of forest trees on the unresting sea.

NOTES

Māmala: Old name for channel entrance to Honolulu har-
bor. The name carried poetic associations of love, as in
one song in which the word contrasts in pun with *mālama*
'to protect': "*Ma ka ʻilikai a o Māmala, mālama ʻia iho ke
aloha,*" 'On the surface of the sea of Māmala, protect the
love' (song, *No ka Pueo*).

Diamond Head: The Hawaiian text gives the old name,
Lēʻahi.

Pearl Harbor hills: The Hawaiian text gives Puʻu-loa,
literally, 'long hills', old name for Pearl Harbor and the
surrounding area.

Piano at Evening

THE COMPOSER, A Hawaiian poet and chanter named Pālea (b. 1852), was a native of Ka'ū, island of Hawai'i. He was already a young man when he went down to a village and heard a piano for the first time. After he arrived home he immediately composed this chant, which soon became popular throughout the Ka'ū region. At one moment he recalls the occasion when he and his wife ("I remember when my dear and I") saw a mirror for the first time aboard the sailing vessel *Nautilus*.

Pālea's younger brother, Kulu-wai-maka, also became known as a poet and musician. He is best remembered as the aged chanter who performed at Lālani Village in Wai-kīkī as late as the 1920s.

❀ ❀ ❀

Piano Ahiahi

'Auhea wale 'oe e piano ahiahi
Hoa 'alo'alo o ke kulu aumoe?

Text: Mary Kawena Pukui

Ho'olono i ka leo o ke kāhuli,
Leo honehone o ka pili o ke ao.

'O 'oe a 'o wau kai 'ike iho
I ke aniani o ka moku *Naukilo*.

Aia i ka luna o Mā'eli'eli
Ka nene'e a ka ua Pō'aihale.

Ha'ina 'ia mai ana ka puana,
Hoa 'alo'alo o ke kulu aumoe.

✿ ✿ ✿

Piano at Evening

O Piano I heard at evening,
where are you?

Your music haunts me far into the night
like the voice of landshells
trilling sweetly
near the break of day.

I remember when my dear and I
visited aboard the *Nautilus*
and saw our first looking glass.

I remember the upland of Maʻeliʻeli
where the mists creeping in and out
threaded their way between the old
houses of thatch.

Again I chant my refrain
of long ago and a piano singing
far into the night.

~~~~~~~~~~~~~~~~~

NOTES

landshells: In the Hawaiian text, this is given as *kāhuli*,
the general name for various land- or tree-shells. Their
sound resembles the chirr of crickets or cicadas. A poetic
name for Hawaiian land-shells was *pūpū-kani-oe*, literally,
'shell that sounds long', so called in the belief that the
"singing" shells had voices.

Māʻeliʻeli: The old-style houses were clustered along the
cindery slopes above Wai-o-hinu.

Bill the Ice Skater

SINCE THE DAYS of Ka-lani-ʻōpuʻu and Ka-
mehameha I, Hawaiians have been great travelers.
"In the period immediately following the discovery
of the islands by Captain Cook," according to Ralph
Kuykendall, "scarcely a ship stopped here without
carrying away one or more Hawaiians, as seamen,
as servants, or, more rarely, as passengers." Here is
a roster of early travelers of distinction, listed by
Kuykendall, whose names figure in Hawaiian history,
or at least in its footnotes:

> The high chief Kaiana, whose travels are detailed in
> the pages of Meares' *Narrative*; the Hawaiian youth
> taken by Delano in 1801 who performed on the theatrical
> stage in Boston in the "Tragedy of Captain Cook," and
> was "much admired by the audience and the publick
> in general"; Opukahaia, whose visit to the United States
> led to such memorable results; George Kaumualii, son
> of the king of Kauai, who was wounded while in the
> United States naval service during the War of 1812;
> finally, King Liholiho and his retinue, who made the
> famous pilgrimage to England. ("An Hawaiian in
> Mexico," p. 37)

Bill the ice skater can hardly be considered to be-
long in such distinguished company. Probably he was
one of the thousands of forgotten seamen, servants,

cattle hands, and common laborers who sometimes returned from their adventures and sometimes did not.

❀ ❀ ❀

Pila, ke Keiki Holohau

Ua hoʻi mai nei ʻo Pila,
He wahi keiki holohau.
I ke kai aku nei oia,
ʻAkāhi nō a hoʻi mai,
Namu mai walawala,
Pakakē launa ʻole!

Wahi ana "Mi no hao!"

Hī noluea a i nolea.

Haʻina mai ka puana
He wahi keiki holohau.

Text: Mary Kawena Pukui

❀ ❀ ❀

Bill the Ice Skater

Bill's home again.
Now he's an ice skater.
Back from his seafaring,
when Bill opens his mouth
the words come a-tumbling—
you never heard such jargon!

"Mi no hao!" says Bill.

Everything jibber-jabber,
jabber-jibber,
pell mell!

This is my song about
Bill the ice skater.

What Is a Boy Like?

T HE LANGUAGE OF the verses at times suggests
that this author was not Hawaiian but a settler of
foreign background, probably American. The for-
eign—"haolified"—flavor of the text arises partly
from the numerous Hawaiianized loan-words:
huila (wheel), *dia* (deer), *wati* (watch), *bele* (bell),
paki (pace), *hipa* (sheep).

❀ ❀ ❀

Ua Like ke Keikikāne me ke Aha?

Me ka nalo nahu
Me ke kani pahu
Me ka 'enuhe kolo
Me ka puhi holo
Me ka lupe lele
Me ka manu mele
Me ka huila ka'a la
Me ka 'ili ma'a la

Me ka pahi olo
Me ka wai nonolo
Me ke dia lele

   Text: Mary Kawena Pukui

Me ka māhu pele
Me ke kai halulu
Me ka lālā ulu
Me ka wati kani
Me ka lama lani

Me ka pū kakani
Me ke aniani
Me ka puke helu
Me ka manu Selu
Me ka mino ʻaka
Me ka hipa laka
Me ka pua ʻula
Me ka hale kula

Me ka bele kani
Me ka moku nani
Me ka lio peki
Me kē o ʻūkēkē
Me ke koʻi lipi
Me ke koa kipi

Me he mau mea nane
Ke keikikāne!

❀ ❀ ❀

What Is a Boy Like?

Like a gnat
like a beating drum
like a crawling caterpillar
like a moving eel
like a flying kite
like a singing bird
like a cart wheel
like a slingshot

Like a saw
like gurgling water
like a leaping deer
like volcanic steam
like a roaring sea
like a growing branch
like a ticking watch
like a heavenly torch

Like a sounding trumpet
like a mirror
like an arithmetic book
like a quail
like a smile
like a gentle sheep
like a red flower
like a schoolhouse

Like a ringing bell
like a beautiful ship
like a pacing horse
like the twang of the ʻūkēkē
like an axe
like a rebellious soldier

Like all of these riddles—
so is a boy!

~~~~~~~~~~~~~~~~

NOTE

ʻūkēkē: A kind of musical bow played by strumming on
strings; the mouth serves as a sound box for resonance.

All the Folks at
'Ula-kōheo

FROM THE EARLY whaling days through the nine-
teenth century numerous Hawaiian sailors shipped
out of Lā-hainā, Hilo, and Honolulu to see something
of the world. Few of these venturesome fellows have
left documentary records of what they saw and how
they felt on their travels, and of how they passed their
time in the foreign ports they visited. An excep-
tion is the anonymous author of *All the Folks at
'Ula-kōheo.*

Like sailors ashore everywhere, he seems to have
spent a good deal of his time strolling about and
taking it easy in the squares, marketplaces, and
plazas of his ports-of-call. His *kāhea*, song of greet-
ing to his Honolulu friends and relations, may be
compared, as a glimpse of the Hispano-American
scene when viewed through Hawaiian eyes, with
Queen Emma's description of Mexican townlife in
a letter of June 7, 1865, to her brother-in-law, King
Ka-mehameha V:

Mexico, Acapulco

Your Majesty

We arrived at this place on the 5th, just a month
from home, and I assure you the sight of land made us
very homesick. We found the U. S. war Steamer
Saranack in port where she has been for 3 months. Like
people who have never left their homes we saw like-
nesses in every cliff, hillock, Palm grove, breeze, etc.,
etc., to places at the Islands.

This is a quaint little town laying in a very pretty
land locked bay, with its roughly paved streets, tiled
houses, dirty plazas, dilapidated Fort and dirty, thin
looking people, not unlike our poorest samples, the
men walking about in large hats and with their sera-
phas [serapes] hanging down from one shoulder and
the women with their scarfs over their heads, and
baskets of fruit on top of it.

Mr Hopkins instantly took a house for us when we ar-
rived and we find it very pleasant, as much so as is pos-
sible to be in this furnice of Acapulco, and I write now
in it—the floor bricked, roof thatched with grass. There
is a nice wide piazza in front and little back garden
the size of my bedroom at home, with an oleander bush
in the center. Its furnishings consists of cotts, a manilla
hammock, and couple of chairs.

The Governor called to see me yesterday with four
of his officers, and a very nice old gentleman he is, ex-
ceedingly courteous but rather infirm. His father is still
living and is 108 years old.

The old Mexicans here all dislike the French rule.
They are expecting their return and intend leaving the
place rather than submit to their rule.

We took a short ride yesterday, and this morning

walked around to look at the place. The people have
been very kind to us. (Queen Emma Collection, Ar-
chives of Hawaii)

In general, Queen Emma found the Latin tempera-
ment of Mexican Spaniards, some French folk (in
1866 she spent three winter months at Hyères in
Provence), and all Italians highly congenial to the
Hawaiian side of her character. If she had met her
seafaring fellow-countryman in the picturesque
plaza in Acapulco, she well might have agreed with
him: "And the people are just the same!"

❀ ❀ ❀

Kō 'Ula-kōheo Po'e

Hū mai ko'u aloha
I kō 'Ula-kōheo po'e.

Ho'omana'o a'e nō au
I ke alanui Nu'u-anu,
Iā Moni-ka-hā'ae ho'i,
Ma kai o Polelewa,
Waiho nā pāpahi lei,
Nā 'ōwili o ka paka,
Nā hīna'i hua manu,
Nā mea a pau loa.

Text: Mary Kawena Pukui

Aia i Akapulako
Kō lākou po'e like.

Ha'ina ka puana
Nō kō 'Ula-kōheo po'e.

❀ ❀ ❀

All the Folks at 'Ula-kōheo

Aloha from Acapulco!
Greetings to all the folks at 'Ula-kōheo.

I keep being reminded here of Nu'u-anu Street
around the Good Eats Restaurant—
also ocean-side of Polelewa
where the lei-bundles are spread out
with the twists of leaf-tobacco
and eggs-for-sale in their country baskets—
anything and everything—

Well, here at Acapulco that's the way it is—
and the people are just the same!

So this is the song I sing
for all the folks at 'Ula-kōheo.

Aloha from Acapulco!

NOTES

ʻUla-kōheo: Vicinity of old Honolulu Iron Works, near
the present Matson docks at the harbor end of Fort Street.

Good Eats Restaurant: This is given in the Hawaiian text
as Moni-ka-hāʻae, literally, 'mouth-watering'; situated
on Hotel near Fort and Bethel streets.

Polelewa: Neighborhood of Nuʻu-anu and King streets,
where peddlers and vendors displayed their wares, espe-
cially for crews of foreign vessels.

Sure a Poor Man

THE SONG IS modeled on the subject matter and stanzaic structure, with prominent refrain, of American work-ballads and marching songs, especially those in the form of autobiographical narrative mixed with social protest. *Pua Mana Nō, 'Sure a Poor Man,'* was written to the tune of *When Johnny Comes Marching Home*. The allusion to the "plantation store" may have been a relatively late addition to the song in its earliest version.

❀ ❀ ❀

Pua Mana Nō

I
I Kahiki au i ka 'imi dālā,
   Dālā pohō.
A holo au ma ka 'ō koholā,
   Koholā lalau.
Ua pau ku'u moku i kāhi kenekoa,
Ua pau ku'u moku i kāhi kenekoa.
Ho'i mai au he pua mana nō,
Ho'i mai au he pua mana nō.

   Text: Mary Kawena Pukui

II

I Ke-kaha au i ka maʻauʻauwā,
   I ka maʻau ʻauwā.
Puehu ka lepo, welawela ka lā,
   Welawela ka lā.
Ua pau kuʻu pono i ka luna ʻauhau,
Ua pau kuʻu pono i ka luna ʻauhau.
Hoʻi mai au he pua mana nō,
Hoʻi mai au he pua mana nō.

III

Nonoke au i ka mahi kō,
   I ka mahi kō.
Ua ʻeha ke kua, kakahe ka hou,
   Pohō, pohō.
A ʻaiʻē au i ka hale kūʻai,
A ʻaiʻē au i ka hale kūʻai.
A noho hoʻi he pua mana nō,
A noho hoʻi he pua mana nō.

IV

A haʻalele au i ka ʻimi dālā,
   Dālā pohō.
E noho nō e hana ma ka lā,
   Ka ʻai o ka lā.
Iā haʻi ka waiwai e luhi ai,
Iā haʻi ka waiwai e luhi ai.
E noho au he pua mana nō,
E noho au he pua mana nō.

✿ ✿ ✿

Sure a Poor Man

I

I went to a foreign land to work for money,
   Wasted money.
Then I went to harpoon whales,
   Worthless whales.
My ship soon belonged to a senator,
My ship soon belonged to a senator.
I came home a poor man,
I came home a poor man.

II

In Ke-kaha I worked as a peddler,
   A peddler was I.
The dust blew up, the sun scorched,
   The sun did scorch and burn.
The tax collector took all my gain,
The tax collector took all my gain.
I came home a poor man,
I came home a poor man.

III

I labored on a sugar plantation,
   Growing sugarcane.
My back ached, my sweat poured,
   All for nothing.

I fell in debt to the plantation store,
I fell in debt to the plantation store.
And remained a poor man,
And remained a poor man.

IV

I decided to quit working for money,
    Money to lose.
Far better work day by day,
    Grow my own daily food.
No more laboring so others get rich,
No more laboring so others get rich.
Just go on being a poor man,
Just go on being a poor man.

NOTE

belonged to a senator: Perhaps an allusion to the com-
mandeering of Northern vessels by the United States
government during the Civil War. But it may also simply
be satiric comment aimed at American congressmen
in general.

Song of the
Chanter Ka-'ehu

Ka-laupapa, around 188–

K A-'EHU, A NATIVE of Kaua'i, was a composer, chanter, and hula master who was active during the reigns of Ka-mehameha V, Luna-lilo, and Ka-lā-kaua. He was noted especially for his speed of invention, being able to compose words, set them to a chant tune, and then perform them in an hour or so. He was markedly original, particularly in his use of vivid figurative language, as well as productive. He frequently drew the subject matter of his poetry from his observations of everyday life in Hawai'i, as when he describes in one chant, for example, belt-operated machinery in motion at the Honolulu Iron Works, or when, in another, he celebrates the inter-island steamer, *Kilauea*, valiantly battling the rough waters of a channel passage with a storm coming on.

The chant is autobiographical. Ka-'ehu became a leper and died at the Ka-laupapa settlement on Moloka'i. This chant is his last known composition.

🌸 🌸 🌸

Mele a Ka-ʻehu ka Haku Mele

E aha ʻia ana o Hawaiʻi
I nei maʻi o ka lēpela,
Maʻi hoʻokae a ka lehulehu
A ka ʻili ʻulaʻula ʻili ke ʻokeʻo?

ʻAno ʻe mai ana nā hoa hui
Like ʻole ka pilina mamua.
He ʻāhiu ke ʻike mai,
Neʻe a kāhi ʻe noho mai,
Kuhikuhi mai hoʻi ka lima,
He maʻi Pākē kō ʻiā ʻla.

Kūlou au a hōʻoiāʻiʻo,
Komo ka hilahila i ka houpo.

Lohe ana kauka aupuni,
Hoʻoūna ke koa mākaʻi.
Hopuhopu ʻia mai kohu moa,
Alakaʻi i ke ala kohu pipi.
Ku ana imua o ka Papa Ola,
Papa ola ʻole o nei maʻi.
Kiʻei wale mai nā kauka,
Hālō maʻō, maʻaneʻi,

Text: Mary Kawena Pukui

Kuhi a'e na lima i Lē'ahi,
"Hele 'oe ma Kalawao."

Lālau nā koa Aupuni,
Halihali iā kai ka uwapo.
Ho'īli nā pio a pau,
Ka luahi i ka ma'i lēpela.
Hiki ke aloha kaumaha nō
I ka 'ike 'ole i ka 'ohana.
Ka waimaka ho'i ka 'elo'elo,
Ho'opulu i ka pāpālina.
Pau ka 'ikena i ka 'āina
I ka wehiwehi o ke kaona.

Hao wikiwiki iā lilo ho'i,
Kū ka huelo i ke kia mua,
E nonoho lua 'o *Keoni Pulu,*
Kīpū i ka hoe mahope,
Ho'ohū ka helena o ke kai,
A he pipi'i wale mai nō.
'Ike iā Moloka'i mamua
Ua pōwehiwehi i ka noe.

Ha'ina mai ka puana
Nō nei ma'i o ka lēpela.

❀ ❀ ❀

Song of the Chanter Ka-'ehu

What will become of Hawai'i?
What will leprosy do to our land—
disease of the despised, dreaded alike
by white or brown or darker-skinned?

Strange when a man's neighbors
become less than acquaintances.
Seeing me they drew away.
They moved to sit elsewhere, whispering,
and a friend pointed a finger:
"He is a leper."

I bowed my head.
I knew it was true.
In my heart I hugged my shame.

Word reached the medical authorities.
The doctors sent the military to fetch us.
We were caught like chickens, like cattle herded
along roadway and country lane.
Then they paraded us before the Board of Health
but there was no health in that Board for such as we.
Examining doctors eyed us, squinted this way and
    that.
More fingers pointed Diamond Head way:
"You go to Kala-wao!"

Again the militia took over.
Soldiers escorted us to the wharf for farewell.
Prisoners, we were marched aboard,
victims of leprosy, branded for exile.
Abandoned, cut off from family and dear ones,
we were left alone with our grief, with our love.
Rain of tears streamed from leper eyes.
Leper cheeks glistened with raindrops in the sun.
Never again would we look upon this land of ours,
this lovely harbor town.

Quickly the sails were hoisted.
Ropes dangled from the foremast,
tails of wild animals writhing,
whipping in the channel breeze.
The *John Bull* drew anchor.
In the stern the rudder turned.
So sailed we forth to dim Moloka'i Island,
enshrouded in fog.

So ends my song and this refrain.
What will leprosy do to my people?
What will become of our land?

NOTE

The *John Bull*: In the Hawaiian text, this is given as *Keoni Pulu*, the Hawaiian name for the *Warwick*, an interisland sailing ship used frequently during later decades of the nineteenth century for transporting lepers to Moloka'i. Finding the English word *Warwick* unfamiliar and unpronounceable, Hawaiians preferred an easier and still appropriate name.

The Love of God

T HE VERSES ARE based on 1 Corinthians, chapter
13: "Though I speak with the tongues of men and
of angels, and have not charity, I am become as
sounding brass, or a tinkling cymbal." The four
stanzas are paraphrases in Hawaiian primarily of
verses 4, 5, 6, and 13:

> Charity suffereth long, and is kind; charity envieth
> not; charity vaunteth not itself, is not puffed up,
> Doth not behave itself unseemly, seeketh not her
> own, is not easily provoked, thinketh no evil;
> Rejoiceth not in iniquity, but rejoiceth in the truth;
> ...
> And now abideth faith, hope, charity, these three;
> but the greatest of these is charity.
> *King James Version*

❀ ❀ ❀

Ke Aloha o ke Akua

Ke aloha o ke Akua
'A'ole ho'i e ho'ohiehie,
'A'ole he hikiwawe ka huhū,
'A'ole no'ono'o 'ino.

Text: Mary Kawena Pukui

O ke aloha o ke Akua
'A'ole pāonioni ke aloha,
'A'ole ha'anui aku ke aloha,
'A'ole he ha'akei.

O ke aloha o ke Akua
'A'ole ia he ho'opunipuni,
'A'ole 'imi i kona mea iho,
'A'ole he kua'aku'ai.

Ke mau nei keia mau mea,
Ka mana'o'i'o, ka mana'olana,
A me ke aloha o ke Akua,
Ke aloha na'e ka i 'oi.

❀ ❀ ❀

The Love of God

Love that is of God
Is not full of vanity,
Is not quick to anger,
Nor thinketh evil to any man.

Love that is of God
Is love without strife,
Is love that vaunteth not itself,
Is humble and not puffed up.

Love that is of God
Is without deceptions,
Seeketh not its own,
Giveth not to receive.

These things still abide,
Faith and hope and the love
That is of God: and of these
Love is the greatest.

Fire Chant for
King Ka-lā-kaua

O'ahu, 1874

IN PRE-CHRISTIAN HAWAI'I the burning of torches
by day was kapu, a sanction, possessed only by
certain royal chiefs. According to tradition, the fire-
burning kapu originated with a high chief of the
island of Hawai'i during the sixteenth century. This
semilegendary ruler, Iwi-kau-i-ka-ua, was a great-
great-grandson of the famous King 'Umi. Later
rulers of the Ka-mehameha and Ka-lā-kaua families
regarded Iwi-kau-i-ka-ua as the ancestor through
whom they inherited the right to burn torches by
day. Iwi-kau-i-ka-ua's wife, a woman of the highest
rank, detested equally her husband's mother and his
daughter born to him by a union with his sister.
When Iwi-kau-i-ka-ua learned that his wife had
brought about the murder of his mother and daugh-
ter, he deserted her and set out with his retinue on
a tour of Hawai'i, keeping his funeral torches alight
both night and day. As a result of his grief-stricken
journey of revenge—"burning, burning, by day
and by night"—the right to burn torches by day be-
came a sacred kapu of his descendants.

During the opening decades of the nineteenth
century, the fire-burning kapu was one of the rights
handed down from ruler to ruler among the Ha-
waiian kings descended from Ka-mehameha I and
his ancestors. Later when David Ka-lā-kaua was
elected king of Hawai'i in 1874, he wanted espe-
cially to strengthen the belief that his claim to the
throne rested on more than man-made agencies and
mere constitutional procedures. To burn torches
by day became under Ka-lā-kaua again a highly sig-
nificant symbolic act expressive of the king's sacred
power, his *mana*.

This was not the only royal kapu belonging to Ka-
lā-kaua's line. He could also claim the hereditary
power to compel subjects, including lesser chiefs,
"to bow down full on the ground"—in other words,
to prostrate themselves at his feet. By 1874, how-
ever, the feasibility of glorifying a Hawaiian mon-
arch by invoking the humiliating prostration kapu
was definitely out of the question. This was not so
with the fire-burning kapu, a spectacular custom that
easily lent itself to the pageantry and excitement
of political demonstrations even under a constitu-
tional monarchy. There is no doubt that the organized
burning of torches in Hawai'i under Ka-lā-kaua was
in part a revivification of ancient Hawaiian practice;
but it was also in imitation of the prevailing Western
taste for staging sensational torchlight processions
to arouse political enthusiasm, as in American
presidential campaigns.

The *Fire Chant for King Ka-lā-kaua* was one of
the first chants composed expressly in honor of David
Ka-lā-kaua about the time of his succession to the
throne in 1874. Though he had been elected to serve
as king by a sizable majority of the Hawaiian Legis-
lature, his political position at the outset of his reign
was far from secure. On the very day of his triumph,
several hundred supporters of the rival candidate,
the Dowager Queen Emma, rioted at the scene of
the election, both inside and outside the courthouse.
Because of this disturbance, Ka-lā-kaua and his
friends hastily decided to forestall further risks of
civil disorder. Indeed, there would be no showy
celebration of his accession to the throne until well
after the new king had been sworn into office in some
quietly safe and unobtrusive way.

After conferring with his leading advisors (sev-
eral of them now members of his first cabinet), Ka-
lā-kaua came to the conclusion that a royal progress
through the kingdom would be the best device for
allowing the dust to settle in the capital while con-
solidating grass-roots support for his new dynasty.
Ka-lā-kaua's first royal tour through his kingdom
began in the second half of March, with a visit to
Kaua'i as stately prelude, and continued through
a good part of April, culminating in ever more and
more popular visits to rural O'ahu. He was loyally
welcomed on all three main outlying islands with
the customary speech-making in Hawaiian and

English, hymn-singing, traditional chanting, present-
ing of leis and other offerings, interspersed with
frequent feasts and bouts of liquid refreshment.
(The visit to the leper settlement at Ka-laupapa on
Moloka'i had important political overtones, but it
was not made a festal occasion.) A marked feature
of several of the public demonstrations, especially
on Maui, was an elaborate fireworks display, not
only in the familiar form of rockets and Roman
candles, but enhanced by grand bonfires blazing
simultaneously from beach and headland and by
torches burning both night and day.

The *Pacific Commercial Advertiser*, on April 4,
pronounced that the water-and-fire pageantry at
Lā-hainā, Maui, had been stupendous.

A little before three o'clock in the morning, as soon
as the *Kilauea* became visible, a large number of bon-
fires were lighted along the shore, from Shaw's Point in
Kaanapali, to Ukumehame beach, while high up the
mountain, overlooking the landscape, was the largest
bonfire of all, which shone like a perfect gem set in the
mountainside, say 3,000 feet above the sea.... Mean-
while, the Court House was illuminated and a line of
burning torches, held by willing and eager hands, ar-
ranged in close order along the beach from the near
residence of His Excellency P[aul] Nahaolelua to the
point beyond the lighthouse. Next came a procession of
boats, nearly thirty in number, each illuminated by from
four to ten torches, moving in single file out of the har-
bor to meet the steamer. As soon as the latter had an-

chored, the boats formed a circle around the ship and,
after a couple of Hawaiian airs had been sung by chosen
singers, three cheers were given for the King. . . .

The *Fire Chant for King Ka-lā-kaua* commemo-
rates the civic welcome given Ka-lā-kaua by his peo-
ple on Oʻahu upon the *Kilauea*'s return to Honolulu
on April 14. The chant was doubtless performed on
later occasions during his torch-lit reign. The orig-
inal text of the chant, published in Honolulu on
April 21, was composed by a young supporter of
Ka-lā-kaua, who was employed as assistant editor
of *Nuhou* (*The News*), a bilingual newspaper edited
and owned by Walter Murray Gibson. With Ka-lā-
kaua safely elected, Gibson almost immediately
abandoned publication of his newspaper, which
had successfully achieved one of its main purposes.
Gibson eventually became King Ka-lā-kaua's pre-
mier and cabinet factotum in his government.

Gibson's editorial assistant, one of whose last
journalistic productions for *Nuhou* was the *Fire
Chant*, also began to play a more overt and active
role in the party politics of the new dynasty. His
name was David Malo and he was a relative (very
probably a nephew) of the David Malo, the erudite
Christianized native who under missionary sponsor-
ship compiled *Hawaiian Antiquities* (*Moolelo
Hawaii*), a valuable source book on pre-Christian
Hawaiian beliefs and customs. David Malo II ac-

companied Ka-lā-kaua on the royal tour round the
islands. His chant appears to have been composed
and sent to the press within a period of hours after
the king landed at Honolulu.

While Ka-lā-kaua on Maui and Hawai'i was pre-
senting his ideas about Hawai'i's future to the local
population, the king's party and its well-wishers on
O'ahu meanwhile outdid themselves to assure a right
royal welcome at home. According to newspaper
announcements, Major William Luther Moehonua,
formerly court chamberlain under the Ka-mehameha
kings and a chanter and poet of note, had been in
charge of organizing pyrotechnical displays (with
the help of the royal militia) and encouraging in-
terest in public manifestations of loyalty. The var-
ious bonfires and spectacular fireworks on Punch-
bowl hill identified in the chant are for the most part
described from the point of view of an eyewitness
stationed aboard the *Kilauea* and approaching the
windward coast of O'ahu around nightfall. After
landing at Honolulu harbor, the royal party and its
guests proceeded by carriage or on foot from the
wharf to King Street and into the palace grounds.

After Malo composed his chant for Ka-lā-kaua,
it became under Hawaiian custom a personal pos-
session of the monarch and his descendants, and its
historic authorship was ignored or forgotten. That
the chant exists today is not simply a consequence
of its publication and survival in print. Court chant-

ers by their performances during Ka-lā-kaua's reign
kept their versions of the text alive as part of a
deeply rooted oral tradition that continues to exist
in Hawai'i today, though on a greatly diminished
scale, almost a century after David Malo the younger
wrote down his original composition as part of his
"copy" for *Nuhou*. Indeed, in the early autumn of
1969, the well-known Hawaiian chanter Kaupena
Wong of Honolulu recited a portion of the *Fire
Chant for King Ka-lā-kaua* during a "lighting up"
ceremony at 'Io-lani Palace, in joint celebration
of that enduring symbol of the vanished Hawaiian
Kingdom and the dedication of the handsome modern
state capitol of Hawai'i Nei.

❀ ❀ ❀

He Inoa Ahi nō Ka-lā-kaua

Lamalama i Maka-pu'u ke ahi o Hilo.
Hanohano molale ke ahi o Ka-wai-hoa.
'Oaka 'ōni'o 'ula kāo'o ke ahi i Wai-'alae.
Ho'oluehu iluna ke ahi o Lē'ahi.
Ho'onohonoho i muliwa'a ke ahi o Ka-imu-kī.
Me he uahi koai'e la ke ahi o Wa'ahila.
Noho hiehie ke ahi i pu'u o Mānoa.
Oni e kele i luna ke ahi o 'Uala-ka'a.

Text: Mary Kawena Pukui

A me he ʻahi la ke ahi o Kaluʻ-āhole.
Me he maka-ihu-waʻa la ke ahi o Helu-moa.
Me he moa-lawakea la ke ahi o Kālia.
Me he pāpahi lei la ke ahi o Ka-wai-a-Haʻo.

ʻO mai ke ʼLiʻi nona ia inoa ahi!

Kauluwela i Pū-o-waina ke ahi hōʻike inoa,
Uluwehiwehi ke ahi hoʻokele Hawaiʻi.
Heaha la ia ka pāniʻo o ke ahi? O ka Helu ʻElua.
Pū-ʻulu hōkū-lani ke ahi o Mālia-ka-malu.
A maʻamau pinepine ke ahi o Kawa.
ʻAlua ʻole ke ahi o Moana-lua.
I puʻupuʻua ke ahi ka mauʻu nēnē.
Kaʻi haʻaheo ke ahi puoko ʻula i ka moana.
ʻĀnuenue pipiʻo lua i ka lewa ke ahi o ke kaona.

ʻO mai ke ʼLiʻi nona ia inoa ahi!

Me he papa-kōnane la ke ahi o Alanui Pāpū.
Ahu kīnohinohi ke ahi i Alanui Aliʻi.
Me he pōnaha mahina la ke ahi o Hale Aliʻi.
Ku me he ʻanuʻu la ke ahi o ka pahu hae.
Wela kuʻu ʻāina i ke ahi o ʻIhi-kapu-lani.

ʻO mai ke ʼLiʻi nona ia inoa ahi!

🏵 🏵 🏵

Fire Chant for King Ka-lā-kaua

Torchlight of Hilo lighted his way to Maka-puʻu.
Now Ka-wai-hoa's royal fire burns clear in the Oʻahu
    night.
A throng of red flashing fires of Wai-ʻalae swirl in
    the air.
Lēʻahi's fire scatters to the stars.
Coals banked at sterns of canoes glow in Ka-imu-kī's
    dusky fires.
Smoky fire of Waʻahila rises like scent of acacia,
    aroma of love.
A chieftain pillar of proud fire stands on a Mānoa
    hillside.
Springing fire of ʻUala-kaʻa embraces the sky.
Gleam of *ʻahi*, fish of yellow flame, shines in the fire
    of Kaluʻ-āhole.
Fire of Helu-moa shows phosphorescent, a mirage
    at sea.
White cock, head of white cock lifted in darkness,
    is fire of Kālia.
A great Aliʻi, fire of Ka-wai-a-Haʻo, stands wreathed
    in purest light.

Answer us, O Chief, whose fire chant we sing!

Intense fire spells out his name on Punchbowl Hill.
He is the Helmsman—*Ka Mō'ī*—revealed in flame
  and rockets' glare.
What is that portal of friendly lamplight? Fire
  Company Number Two.
Blessed fires of Mary of Peace shine like a congrega-
  tion of stars.
Fire of constancy is the fire of Kawa, unwavering
  fire.
Bonfires of Moana-lua burn unmatched for wild
  display.
Banks of *nēnē*-grass one after another burst into
  blaze.
So proud warriors tread by torchlight, their march-
  ing mirrored in the sea.
That double rainbow arching the sky is the reflected
  fire of the town.

  Answer us, O Chief, whose fire chant we sing!

A checkered *kōnane*-board is Fort Street on fire.
Gay calico prints are the fires decorating King.
The fire at the Palace shines in a circle, a full moon.
Like a tower atop an ancient temple is the fire-ringed
  flagpole.
So lives my land heated everywhere by the sacred
  kapu-fire of 'Ihi-kapu-lani.

  Answer us, O Chief, whose fire chant we sing!

≈≈≈≈≈≈≈≈≈

NOTES

Maka-puʻu: Rugged point on coast of Oʻahu east of Hono-
lulu. The name (literally, 'hill beginning') also suggests
"bulging eye," said to be the name of an image found in
a cave in the cliff face. The image represented a legendary
woman called Maka-puʻu who, with her sister, came in
ancient times to Oʻahu—"where we can see the cloud drifts
of Kahiki."

Ka-wai-hoa: Point beyond Portlock Road east of Hono-
lulu, literally, 'the companion's water'; in early times
much used as a place of anchorage.

Wai-ʻalae: Approximately the same as the present Wai-
ʻalae-Kahala section of Honolulu, but originally the
name of an *ahupuaʻa*, land division extending from the
uplands to the sea. The name (literally, 'mudhen water')
refers to a spring or springs and their streams flowing from
various elevations, especially the summits of Wai-ʻalae-nui
and Wai-ʻalae-iki. In the 1870s, despite introduced dis-
eases and epidemics, the region was still well populated
with Hawaiian farmers and fisherfolk, though not so dense-
ly as in the eighteenth century.

Lē-ʻahi: Variant of Lae-ʻahi, old name for Diamond Head.
The profile was compared by Hiʻi-aka to the brow (*lae*)
of the *ʻahi*, yellowfin tuna.

Ka-imu-kī: Roughly the same as the section of Honolulu
now so known, originally an *ahupuaʻa*. The name (lit-
erally, 'the ti oven') carried associations with the Mene-
hune, the legendary race of small people who built ovens
by night.

Waʻahila: Section between Mānoa and Nuʻu-anu valleys;
also name for a gentle wind and rain. Said to be named
for a chiefess who became famous for her alluring dance
of the same name.

Koaiʻe, in the Hawaiian text, is a native acacia with a
particularly pleasant fragrance. Allusions to *koaiʻe* in
poetry sometimes refer to love: "a euphemism," accord-
ing to N. B. Emerson, "for the delicate parts" (*Unwritten
Literature*, p. 68).

Mānoa hillside: In the Hawaiian text this is given as *puʻu
o Mānoa*, and refers to the present Rocky Hill, part of
ancient Mānoa-aliʻi ('chiefs' Mānoa'), a land division
on the western side of a line running from Molokaʻi Hill
(Puʻu-luahine) at the end of Mānoa Valley down to Rocky
Hill.

ʻUala-kaʻa: Early name for Round Top Hill; literally
'rolling sweet potato', alluding to a legend in which a rat
bit a sweet potato causing it to roll down the hill where
it sprouted. Ka-mehameha I owned extensive lands on the
steeps where the sweet potatoes persisted in rolling away.

ʻahi: In the Hawaiian the chant indulges in word-play in-
volving the nearly identical sounds of *ahi* 'fire' and *ʻahi*,
yellowfin tuna. The colors of fire and those of the yellow-
finned silvery fish lend themselves to magical notions of
the fiery spirits present in both.

Kaluʻ-āhole (for Kalua-āhole) : A fishing spot along the
shore of Diamond Head famous for its *āholehole* (*Kuhlia
sandvicensis*).

Helu-moa: Old land division in Wai-kīkī in vicinity of
present Royal Hawaiian Hotel; once the site of an im-

portant *heiau* near a favorite residence of Queen Ka-'ahu-
manu. The name (literally, 'chicken scratch') refers to a
supernatural rooster who sometimes appeared there.

phosphorescent: From *maka-ihu-wa'a* in the Hawaiian
text. Light seen in the water at night that is produced by
luminescent organisms.

head of white cock: A free translation of *moa-lawakea*
'white cock', but the emphasis on the primitive image serves
to heighten the contrast in the next line with the light-
garlanded (*me he pāpahi lei*) steeple of Ka-wai-a-Ha'o
Church.

Kālia: Section of Honolulu in the vicinity of the present
Ala Wai canal and adjacent yacht harbor; in early times this
was a region of fishponds, gardens, and well-beaten trails.

Ka-wai-a-Ha'o: The historic Congregational church and
meetinghouse in central Honolulu at the intersection of
King and Punchbowl streets, designed by Hiram Bing-
ham, pastor, erected by royal authority, and dedicated
on July 21, 1842. In early days often called the "Stone
Church," because it was built of coral blocks from the
harbor, replacing its four grass-thatched predecessors (the
earliest was erected in 1822). The native name, 'the fresh
water pool of Ha'o', was derived from the church's site,
adjacent to an area where in ancient times were ponds
and a kapu stone. Certain highest chiefs were allowed to
bathe in the upper pool or drink where water flowed over
a sacred stone; commoners were permitted to drink only
from below. In 1927 the kapu stone was moved from its
commercial surroundings and deposited within the walls of
Ka-wai-a-Ha'o Church.

Punchbowl Hill: The old name of this volcanic hill and
extinct crater about five hundred feet above sea level and

overlooking central Honolulu was Pū-o-waina. A cannon bat-
tery was maintained there for saluting vessels, honoring
royalty on birthdays, solemnizing funerals, and so forth.
The hill was long used as a post and training ground for
the Hawaiian militia, both infantry and cavalry. The
Hawaiian name (literally, 'hill of placing') referred to
its ancient use as an amphitheater for human sacrifices,
rituals in which victims were burned to death. Now the
site of the National Memorial Cemetery of the Pacific.

Helmsman: This is given in the Hawaiian text as *hoʻokele*,
'steersman', one who heads affairs. An observer aboard
the *Kilauea* representing the *Pacific Commercial Ad-
vertiser*, April 18, 1874, noted that "Looming high above
and away at the rear, was Punchbowl, its highest peak
surmounted with a blazing crown, forty feet from the
ground, beneath which in letters of fire were the words
Ka Moʻi ['The King']."

Fire Company Number Two: The building was the head-
quarters of Engine Company Number Two, one of several
stations housing equipment of the Honolulu Fire Depart-
ment. At the time of his election Ka-lā-kaua had been a
member of Engine Company Number Four for about thir-
teen years.

Mary of Peace: Our Lady of Peace, the present Roman
Catholic cathedral on Fort Street, a stone church erected
from 1840–1843, following the arrival of a small band
of Catholic missionary priests in 1840. Religious toleration
had been first positively adopted as a policy of the Hawaiian
Government in 1839.

Kawa: The bonfires at Kawa in the harbor area were the
tribute of His Majesty's loyal prisoners at Iwilei Prison.

Moana-lua: Land division and stream west of Honolulu
in vicinity of present Fort Shafter.

nēnē-grass: Piles of *'ai-a-ka-nēnē (Coprosma ernodeoides)*,
a native, woody, trailing plant, became blazing mounds,
easily replenished by the prisoners.

kōnane-board: *Papa-kōnane* in the Hawaiian text, a checker-
board. *Kōnane* was an ancient game similar to checkers,
played with pebbles on a lined stone or board.

calico prints: This is given in the Hawaiian text as *kīno-
hinohi* 'decorated', 'printed, as calico'. The Hawaiian text
suggests the profusion of commercial goods (*ahu* 'heap',
compare *ho'āhu* 'storehouse') characteristic of the busi-
ness quarter.

the Palace: Not the present 'Io-lani Palace constructed
during Ka-lā-kaua's reign (dedicated 1879) as a symbol
of the majesty and elegance of his dynasty, but the "Old
Palace," a modest one-story affair in bungalow style, built
of coral blocks with a lookout on top. Governor Ke-ku-
ana-o'a built the house for his daughter, Victoria Ka-māmalu,
in the 1840s. After 1843, when Ka-mehameha III moved
the seat of government from Lā-hainā, Maui, to Honolulu,
the house became the official royal residence (Hale Ali'i)
of the Ka-mehameha kings, used especially for diplomatic
audiences, state receptions, and formal dinners.

circle, a full moon: A spacious circular drive faced the
"Old Palace" on its King Street side. The comparison
of the fires with the full moon (*pōnaha mahina*, 'round
moon') probably refers to an arrangement of *kukui* torches
bordering the drive.

'Ihi-kapu-lani: Name of a former house on the palace
grounds, near the old banyan tree and present Archives

of Hawaiʻi. King Ka-lā-kaua and Queen Ka-piʻo-lani took
up residence, somewhat ostentatiously in the eyes of their
critics, in the house shortly after their election. The name
of the house, 'hallowed royal kapu', associates the house
with the fire-burning kapu, as does the mention in *Kuokoa*,
April 18, of its appearance on the night of the royal party's
arrival by carriage after landing from the tour: "Before
the door of ʻIhi-kapu-lani house were lights in the form
of a crown and above that were decorations used in an-
cient times. Upon a roof was a fire container kept burn-
ing by a handsome youth."

The Pearl

THE CHANT WAS composed by King Ka-lā-kaua
and addressed to his people in October-November
1881, after his return from a journey to encircle
the world. He had embarked from Honolulu on the
City of Sydney on January 20 of that year, the first
reigning monarch to undertake and accomplish such
a mission. During his magnificent welcome in Japan,
where he and his party spent two weeks as guests of
Emperor Mutsuhito (reign name, Meiji), he also
visited Kobe, Osaka, Kyoto, and Nagasaki. He next
saw something of the Chinese port cities of Shanghai,
Tientsin, and Hong Kong, before continuing on to
Siam, the Malay States, and Burma. In India he
spent only a few days at Calcutta and Bombay,
traveling across the subcontinent by railroad; he
then boarded a steamer for Egypt, the Suez, and
Alexandria. After four months of Oriental travel
the king returned to the Western world by way of
Naples, where he exchanged visits with King Humbert. The pope granted Ka-lā-kaua a pleasant interview at the Vatican in Rome. The Hawaiian party
arrived in London during the first week of July and
was elaborately entertained by Queen Victoria and
prominent representatives of the nobility, government, and church. William N. Armstrong, the king's

attorney general, who tended to disparage foreign
aristocracies, wrote to a colleague in Honolulu:

> I desire to assure you that the many persons who have
> met His Majesty, since His arrival here, express them-
> selves as highly pleased with His Majesty's appearance,
> bearing and intelligence, and I am compelled to believe
> that this visit is of great advantage to the Hawaiian Is-
> lands in creating a just and proper idea of the civiliza-
> tion of that country. (Kuykendall, *Hawaiian Kingdom*,
> p. 233)

The later months of the royal tour took the king
back to the continent, to Belgium, Austria, France,
Spain, and Portugal. He met heads of state in only
two of these countries, Prince William (later Kaiser
William II) in Berlin, and the Archduke Albrecht
in Austria. After his arrival in New York City, Ka-
lā-kaua went to Washington where he was greeted
by President Chester A. Arthur, recent successor to
President James A. Garfield. Garfield was shot on
July 2, 1881, by an assassin, Charles I. Guiteau,
a disappointed office seeker, and died on September
19. The death by assassination of President Gar-
field was not forgotten by King Ka-la-kaua, and there
can be no doubt that he remembered the assassina-
tion of Abraham Lincoln and had read of the several
attempts on the life of Queen Victoria.

Ka-lā-kaua left San Francisco on October 22 on
the steamer *Australia* and on October 29 arrived in

Honolulu, where he received an enthusiastic wel-
come lasting several days. The king's return to his
country had been heralded on October 29 in the
Pacific Commercial Advertiser, whose editor, Wal-
ter Murray Gibson, was the king's premier.

> Kalakaua, by his world-wide range and observation, has
> acquired the character of a cosmopolitan King; and
> it will be fitting, as his beneficent Government har-
> monizes and assimilates with the Archipelago the people
> of Europe and America, and of China, Japan, Hindu-
> stan, and other countries, that Kalakaua shall become
> the Sovereign of a glorious cosmopolitan Pacific state.

A week later, November 5, the same newspaper an-
nounced: "What a contrast for His Majesty between
the October of 1880, and the October of 1881":

> Then distrust, misrepresentation, and much disloyalty
> in certain quarters; though the heart of the people was
> true at the time. Now all loyalty and enthusiasm, and
> mottoes dictated by the warmest and highest regard for
> a Sovereign, met the royal gaze at every side.

❀ ❀ ❀

Ka Momi

Ua kaʻahele au maluna o ka ʻili honua me nā moana,
A ʻInia mamao me Kina kaulana,
Hōʻea i nā ʻae kai o Aferika a me nā palena o Europa,
A hālāwai me ka ikaika o nā ʻāina a pau.

A iaʻu i kū ai ma nā ʻaoʻao o nā poʻo aupuni,
Ka poʻe mana maluna o lākou me ka hiehie,
Hoʻomaopopo iho la au i ka ʻuka iki a nāwaliwali o
   koʻu,
Me koʻu noho aliʻi i hoʻokahua ʻia maluna o kāhi puʻu
   pele,
A ma kāhi he miliona i hoʻokō i ka keia mau mōʻī,
He mau tausani wale nō malalo o koʻu malu.

Akā, ke ʻupu nei loko, naʻu ke kaena hiki,
Aia he mau nani maloko o nā pōʻai o koʻu mau ʻae
   kai,
I ʻoi aku ka makamae i ka oʻu mau hoa aliʻi.
ʻAʻohe oʻu kumu hopo maloko o koʻu aupuni.

He hiki ke hui me koʻu lāhui me ka weli ʻole.
ʻAʻohe makaʻu noʻu iho, me ke kiaʻi paʻa ole ia.

Text: Mary Kawena Pukui. Title assigned.

A naʻu ke kaena, he momi i hoʻoūna ʻia mai luna mai
   naʻu,
Eia me aʻu ke aloha pili paʻa o koʻu lāhui kānaka.

❀ ❀ ❀

The Pearl

I have traveled over many lands and distant seas,
to India afar and China renowned.
I have touched the shores of Africa and the boundaries
   of Europe,
and I have met the great ones of all the lands.

As I stood at the side of heads of governments,
next to leaders proud of their rule, their authority
   over their own,
I realized how small and weak is the power I hold.
For mine is a throne established upon a heap of lava.
They rule where millions obey their commands.
Only a few thousands can I count under my care.

Yet one thought came to me of which I may boast,
that of all beauties locked within the embrace of
   these shores,
one is a jewel more precious than any owned by my
   fellow monarchs.
I have nothing in my Kingdom to dread.

I mingle with my people without fear.
My safety is no concern, I require no bodyguards.
Mine is the boast that a pearl of great price has fallen
    to me from above.
Mine is the loyalty of my people.

Feather Chants for Queen Ka-piʻo-lani

THE TWO CHANTS are from a set of three, commemorating a visit of Queen Ka-piʻo-lani to Rose Mount (Mauna Loke), the residence and sugar plantation owned by John A. Cummins at Wai-mānalo, Oʻahu. According to oral tradition, the chants were presented to the queen, along with accompanying feather leis, early in 1883, the year when King Ka-lā-kaua and the queen were crowned on February 12.

However, Ka-piʻo-lani undoubtedly visited the plantation and Cummins' flower gardens and grounds on a number of occasions, such as when on her birthday, December 31, 1885, she and "quite a number of ladies and gentlemen had been invited from Honolulu, some of whom went by the steamer *Waimanalo*, leaving early in the morning, and others took the overland route later in the day" ("Sugar History," here and following quoted passages). The sea was reported smooth and the journey as a whole was in no way strenuous: "The distance from the landing to Mr. Cummins's residence, over two miles, through sugar cane in all stages of growth, was traveled by the rail."

Only a generation before it became a sugar planta-
tion, the Cummins ranch at Wai-mānalo had been
crown land first leased by Ka-mehameha III in the
1840s to Thomas A. Cummins, an English settler.
The region at that time was still one of heavy forests
and small farms, mainly breadfruit, mountain
apple, *kukui*, and coconut trees, with scores of taro
patches, sweet potato gardens, and fields of native
sugarcane grown solely for domestic use. Grass
houses abounded by the hundreds. Fishing was good
along the shore. After the arrival of Cummins, small
kuleana, customary holdings of old native families,
were sold or abandoned and much of the land was
given over to raising livestock: "Taro patches were
trodden down, edible cane and ti were disturbed,
the large trees died because of lack of moisture for
their roots, and the whole valley became a vast cattle
ranch."

Under the management of Thomas's son, John A.
Cummins, an amiably enterprising part-Hawaiian
who was a good friend of King Ka-lā-kaua, sugar
became the dominant crop in place of sheep, cattle,
and horses; pasture land "gave way to canefield and
racing track to plantation village." The passage of
the Reciprocity Treaty in 1875 quickly made sugar
profitable, and by 1879 the plantation was a going
commercial concern featuring many modern im-
provements. In addition to increasing irrigation
facilities, John A. Cummins imported from Scot-

land a two-roller, eight-ton mill with a capacity of
producing from eight to ten tons of sugar a day. By
January of 1881 grinding had started, and it must
have been these "grinders that falter not at their
grinding" that Ka-piʻo-lani beheld for the first time
shortly before her birthday on December 31, 1882.
Financial control of the plantation and mill passed
into the hands of W. G. Irwin, a very large-scale
operator, in 1885. Cummins continued as local
manager. Gradually Chinese and other Oriental
laborers replaced the native population as the major
source of labor supply.

Clearly the pace of change and modernization
in Hawaiʻi, especially as measured by the intro-
duction of machines, increased in the 1880s. On Janu-
ary 27, 1883, the *Pacific Commercial Advertiser*
noted that "the railway [at Wai-mānalo] is now
finished from the mill to the beach and everything is
in first rate order for growing and securing each
season's crop." In 1883, "telephonic calls" on Oʻahu,
not only in Honolulu but also in the Wai-mānalo
area, were already so numerous that the Bell Tele-
phone Company in September notified its customers
that "the monthly rates will be reduced to $5.00 for
business places and $4.00 for private residences"
(*Pacific Commercial Advertiser*, September 22,
1883).

Earlier in that year the public generally were
advised that "the telephone is a great convenience,

but when one is busy it is rather aggravating and
inclined to make one utter some forcible adjectives
when rung up half a dozen times within a quarter
of an hour, and no one answers you. The mystery is
cleared up by calling the 'Central' who will inform
you it was a mistake" (*Pacific Commercial Adver-
tiser*, March 17, 1883).

❀ ❀ ❀

He Mele Hulu nō Ka-pi‘o-lani i Wai-mānalo

Aia i Wai-mānalo kō nu‘a hulu,
E haku ia mai la e Mololani.

Noho ‘o kalani hano i ka nani,
I ka lawe ha‘aheo a Moku-lua.

Ho‘ohihi ka mana‘o e ‘ike aku,
E kilohi i ka nani o Moku-manu.

Pōhai a ka manu i ka lewa lani,
Kīkahakaha mai i ka ‘ili kai.

Welo ha‘aheo kō hae kalaunu,
‘Ike mai ‘o Mālei ke kupua.

   Text: Mary Kawena Pukui

O ia kai kapu la ua noa,
Ua hehi kū ia aku e kalani.

Nāu i ʻōlali hoʻohie aku,
O ia mau ʻale hānupanupa.

ʻIniki welawela, a ke ʻehu kai,
Lamalama ʻula i ka lani aliʻi.

Liʻliʻi nā hana a ke kelepona,
Haʻihaʻi ʻōlelo me ka huapala.

E Ka-piʻo-lani la e ō mai,
Ka wahine nona ke lei hoʻoheno.

❀ ❀ ❀

A Feather Chant for Ka-piʻo-lani at Wai-mānalo

Now at Wai-mānalo your heap of feathers and our
      offering,
gifts fashioned for you by the people of Mololani.

She sits, the beautiful Chiefess, in her place of honor
journeying onward to Moku-lua.

Entrancing thoughts fill the mind
when eyes mirror Moku-manu's charm.

Birds circle about the sky, poise
in dipping flight over the waves.

Proudly the royal flag flies acknowledged,
greeted by Mālei, guardian goddess of this shore.

Now the sacred kapu of the sea is lifted,
made free by the Chiefess in her journey.

It is she who glides in beauty
over billows of the ever-surging sea.

Cold spray pierces, the skin of the Chiefess warms
    within
from its own ruddy glow.

Now that the telephone makes work such a trifle,
how easy to converse with the best beloved!

O Ka-piʻo-lani, answer to our call!
You are the woman we praise, this lei of affection
    is yours.

〰〰〰〰〰

NOTES

Moku-lua: Two islets off Lani-kai.

Moku-manu: 'Bird-island', islet off Mō-kapu. The Mō-kapu
region, in the Koʻolau-poko division, was a sacred kapu

area, as the name indicates. A native myth claimed it as the place where the first man was created by Kāne, Lono, and Kū.

Mālei: A demigoddess (*kupua*) believed to have migrated to Oʻahu from Kahiki. A stone image at one time stood in back of Maka-puʻu Point, facing the windward side of the island. She was the guardian of the *uhu* or parrotfish that frequented the sea there. The stone has long since disappeared.

❀ ❀ ❀

He Mele Hulu nō Ka-piʻo-lani i Mololani

Aia i Mololani kō nuʻa hulu,
Kāhiko kapu iā nou e kalani.

Onaona nā maka ke ʻike aku,
Hoʻmāhie luna ua liʻa loko.

Ka mākou lani ʻihi nō ʻoe,
Puīa ke ʻala i Mauna Loke.

Ka mālamalama o ke ahi kao,
Ke kahua kolokē hone i ke anu.

Ilaila mākou ʻike i ka nani,
I ka hale wili kō helu ʻekāhi.

Nome hala ʻole mai a ka nau,
Haulani nā pana i ka mīkini.

Pipiʻi a ka māhu o ka moʻa ia,
Pau pono nā ʻono a ka makemake.

O ka noho hoʻolaʻi a ka wahine,
I ka hale aniani o ke kaʻaahi.

Aweawe ka uahi piʻo mahope,
Ka ʻowē a ka lau kō mawaho.

Aia ka ilina i ke ʻehu kai,
I ka hanu līpoa ʻou e kalani.

E Ka-piʻo-lani la e ō mai,
Ka wahine nona ke lei hoʻoheno.

❀ ❀ ❀

A Feather Chant for Ka-piʻo-lani at Mololani

Now at Mololani your heap of feathers and our
    offering,
sacred ornaments for you, O Chiefess.

Your eyes are lovely to behold,
brimming with delight, pleasure speaking to the heart.

Sacred, most truly majestic, you are the Chiefess
whose fragrance now precedes you to Rose Mount.

There sky rockets spill their brightness
over the croquet grounds so alluringly cool.

And at Rose Mount we view the beauty
of the finest of sugar mills.

Now the grinders falter not at their grinding,
and the machine runs always at even speed.

When the steam rises, boiling-time ends.
All sweetness is concentrated there.

The lady in the glassed-in coach
of her train need only sit and relax.

Smoke weaves and streams behind
while leaves of sugarcane rustle outside.

End of the ride is where the salt spray flies,
delicious breath of seaweed, O Chiefess,
    will be yours to inhale!

O Ka-piʻo-lani, answer to our call!
You are the woman we praise, this lei of affection
    is yours.

The Cherished One

T HE CHANT WAS composed by Ka-lā-kaua in November 1890 as a proclamation announcing the regency of his sister, the heiress apparent, Princess Lili'u-o-ka-lani (Loloku-lani), who as Queen Lili'u-o-ka-lani (1838–1917) succeeded Ka-lā-kaua to the throne and became the last ruler of Hawai'i as an independent kingdom. She reigned only until 1893 when she was deposed in a revolutionary coup led by American residents of Hawai'i, many of whom were citizens of the Kingdom. Failing in her counter-revolutionary attempt to overthrow the Provisional Government, she formally renounced her royal claims in 1895. She was the composer of many Hawaiian songs, including *Aloha 'Oe*.

Ka-lā-kaua was in poor health during much of 1890. Hoping to recuperate on the West Coast, he took ship for California on November 25. He died two months later, on January 20, at the Palace Hotel in San Francisco.

The king's body was brought back to Hawai'i on the U.S.S. *Charleston*. Thousands watched the funeral procession when Ka-lā-kaua's coffin was carried to the Royal Mausoleum in Nu'u-anu Valley, Honolulu, on February 15, 1891, where the service of the Anglican church for the burial of the dead was read by Bishop Willis. "The torch that burns at midday," wrote one sensitive observer of the procession and ceremony, "has been quenched" (quoted in Daws, *Shoal of Time*, p. 264).

On the afternoon of January 29, at a meeting of the privy council in Honolulu, attended by the chief justice and chancellor, assisted by associate justices of the supreme court, Liliʻu-o-ka-lani signed and executed the oath prescribed by the Hawaiian constitution. Godfrey Brown, minister of finance, later told the British commissioner, James Hay Wodehouse, that "when he informed Her Majesty that she would have to swear to support the Constitution she showed an evident reluctance to take that step" (Kuykendall, *Hawaiian Kingdom*, p. 474).

🌸 🌸 🌸

Ke Aliʻi Milimili

E ʻike mai ʻoukou.

Nā mokupuni a pau,
Mai ka hikina i Kumu-kāhi
I ka welona i Lehua,
Keia hae kalaunu,
Kapalili nei i ka makani.

Text: Mary Kawena Pukui. Title assigned.

Hanohano kona ʻalo ʻana,
Ka ʻilikai ehuehu.
Pau nā kai ʻewalu
Ka ʻike i kona welo ana,
Nō ka lani kū i ka moku,
Nō Loloku-lani i ke kapu.

Nānā ʻia kō aliʻi,
Kō milimili e Hawaiʻi.

Ka hoʻoilina mōʻī,
O ke kalaunu hanohano.
O ʻoe ka hilinaʻi,
Ke aloha a ka lāhui.

A hoʻi mai o ka lani,
Kau-lī-lua-i-ke-anu,
O kou aupuni.

E ka lani-nānā ia.

❀ ❀ ❀

The Cherished One

Behold, everyone and all!

Let all islands
from the sunrise at Kumu-kāhi

to the sun's rest at Lehua
gaze upon this royal flag
fluttering in the breeze.

This honored flag has journeyed
over oceans in storm.
All eight seas have beheld
this banner in their skies,
waving now for the High Chiefess
who rules over the land:
Loloku-lani, the sacred one.

Look to your Chiefess,
cherish her well, O Hawaiʻi!

She is the royal Princess
wearing majesty's crown.
You, O Chiefess, are the trusted one,
beloved of the people.

Until that day when Kalani,
Kau-lī-lua-i-ke-anu, shall return to these islands
the Kingdom is yours.

O heavenly one, guard it well!

NOTES

Kumu-kāhi: Name of easternmost cape on the island of Hawai'i.

Lehua: Tiny island west of Ni'ihau.

Kau-lī-lua-i-ke-anu: Honorific name for Ka-lā-kaua ('the intense chill lodged in the cold [of Mt. Wai-'ale'ale]'). A chief was sometimes referred to not by his given name but by the first line to appear in a chant that was his personal possession. The appropriate use of such a name was a form of politeness.

The Sprinkler

THE SONG IS attributed to Queen Lili'u-o-ka-lani. According to oral tradition, she was sitting on the *lanai* of Washington Place when she noticed something new to her, a lawn sprinkler, in the yard of her neighbors, Dr. and Mrs. Robert McKibbin. Washington Place was the old family home of her husband, Governor John Dominis, whom she named prince consort in 1891 shortly before the fall of the monarchy. In 1922, a few years after the old queen's death, Washington Place became the official residence of the governors of Hawai'i; it continues to be so to this day.

Ka Wiliwiliwai

> E ka wiliwiliwai,
> Ko'iawe i ka la'i.
> A he aha kāu hana
> E naue mālie nei?

Text: Samuel H. Elbert and Samuel A. Keala, *Conversational Hawaiian*, p. 197.

HUI

Ei nei! Ei nei!

(nā kāne)   Ea— ea—

Ke poahi mai nei

Āhea— Āhea

(nā kāne)   ʻOe— ʻoe

ʻOe kāohi mai.

Oki pau ʻoia ala,

Ua ninihi ka lawena.

Kuʻu iki iho hoʻi

I inu aku au.

The Sprinkler

O whirly-water

gentle rain shower on the move

what do you think you're up to

circling, twirling so quietly?

CHORUS

You there! You there!

(bass)   Yea, yea— coming up!

(hips swinging)   As you revolve,

when— oh, when

(bass)   will you— will you—

will you ever hold still?

Amazing
the way you take over: irresistible.
Come, slow down a little—
so I can drink!

Pele Raped

T
HE SELECTION IS an excerpt (the three closing
sections) from a long chant, in chapter 23 of N. B.
Emerson's *Pele and Hi'iaka*, entitled *The Lame
Fishermen—His Epic Recital Celebrating Pele*.
When the chapter opens, Hi'i-aka, favorite younger
sister of Pele, has almost completed her journey to
find Lohi'au, chief of Kaua'i, in order to escort him
to Pele on the island of Hawai'i, where the volcano
goddess wishes to "spend five days and five nights"
with Lohi'au as her lover. After numerous adven-
tures by sea and land, Hi'i-aka has arrived at Hā'ena
on Kaua'i where she is welcomed by Malae-ha'a-koa,
a fisherman and minor chief who has the power of
prophecy. Malae-ha'a-koa is crippled, and his wife,
Wai-lua-nui-a-hō'ano, has had to carry him down
to the shore. When he meets Hi'i-aka, the lame fisher-
man "divines" that the beautiful visitor is a member
of the Pele family, whereupon through Hi'i-aka's
magical presence and her recital of several spells—
"Send fish, O gods, to the fisherman"—he is in-
stantly cured of his lameness. To show their grati-
tude, Malae-ha'a-koa and his wife immediately
make preparations for a great feast:

When the repast was nearing its end and the people had
well eaten, Malae-haʻa-koa and his wife stood forth
and led in the performance of a sacred dance, accom-
panying their rhythmic motions with a long mele that
recited the deeds, the events, the mysteries that had
marked Pele's reign since the establishment of her
dominion in Hawaii. (p. 112)

The sacred chant forms a sequence of fifteen
sections, each ending with a conventional refrain:
" *ʻEliʻeli, kau mai*," translated in the *Hawaiian
Dictionary* as "May a profound reverence alight
[solemn supplication at the end of prayers]."

Beginning with Pele's stormy departure from
Kahiki accompanied by members of her family and
other divine dignitaries, the chant goes on to describe
in a series of visionary scenes Pele's arrival at suc-
cessive islands, including Kauaʻi and Molokaʻi, and
her eventual landing on the island of Hawaiʻi.

The later portions of the fisherman's chant concern
an early episode of Pele's history on Hawaiʻi: her
relations with a demigod, Kama-puaʻa, who is able to
change himself from a hog to a man and back again
at will. On hearing of the goddess' arrival at the
volcano, Kama-puaʻa had journeyed from his home
island, Oʻahu, to Kīlauea crater on Hawaiʻi. Un-
observed by the goddess, he had watched the fire
dance of Pele and her sisters in the crater. He was
discovered when one of Pele's sisters saw him in the
form of a handsome man dancing by himself high

upon the lip of the fiery caldron to the sound of a
small hand drum.

The chant does not narrate all these exact details
from the Pele-Kama-puaʻa legends. In fact the style
of the chant as a whole is elliptical, gnomic, delib-
erately "dark," sometimes suggesting much more
than it actually states. The language is unusually
dense with allusion, metaphor, and symbol. The
composer of the chant (or its performer in the 1880s
or 1890s, for that matter) could assume that an elite
audience would be thoroughly familiar with the
general sequence of events and no doubt acquainted
with alternate traditions of the same episode. A note-
worthy feature of the Emerson version of the out-
come of Pele's love affair with the pig-god is the
ironic flavor that pervades this part of the narrative,
a quality heightened perhaps by Emerson himself
because of his own imaginative involvement with the
story as commentator and manipulator of the nar-
rative point of view.

Unlike some other versions of the story, there is
nothing to suggest that Pele became Kama-puaʻa's
wife or that she was even briefly reconciled to him
as a lover. Instead, Pele is represented as a woman
of capricious and selfish character, at once lustful
and cold. Though her rape is described as a defile-
ment, we are given the impression by Emerson that
Pele's fall was what she deserved, or at any rate
that in its consequences it was a "fortunate fall." As

a goddess she remains eternally her restless and
vindictive self, periodically breaking out of her
volcanic chamber and wreaking havoc through the
countryside, until peace returns and the land is
redeemed—temporarily at least—by the regenera-
tive power of the male fertility god, Kū-haili-moe
(Kū-moku-hāliʻi).

It has been suggested that the Pele-Kama-puaʻa
legends may have originated in ancient Hawaiʻi in
some story of political intrigue: "a hidden con-
troversy between the priests of rival divinities" (Beck-
with, *Hawaiian Mythology*, p. 193). Whatever their
complex origin, it is certainly true that popular
stories of Pele told in Hawaiʻi today survive largely
because of their power to entertain and amuse. How-
ever, in the chant of the lame fisherman the reader
may find not only entertainment but also a deeper
significance in a drama in which the two sisters be-
come a symbol of the relation between an old order
that has passed away and a gentler new order that has
barely emerged. Under the old order the will of Pele
had ruled for a while almost supreme "regardless of
the younger, the human, race which is fast peopling
the land that was hers in the beginning." The symbol
and promise of the future order is, of course, in
Emerson's words, "the warm-hearted girl whom we
still love to call Hiʻiaka-i-ka-poli-o-Pele"—the
Hiʻi-aka who had dwelt mysteriously in the breast
of the old woman of the volcano until, by an inde-

pendent act of will, she became a manifestation of
essential womanhood in her own right (*Pele and
Hiʻiaka*, pp. 239–240).

🌼 🌼 🌼

Ka Hana ʻIno iā Pele

I

Ua lili ka lani me ka ua;
Ua oʻoki ka lani, pōʻele ka honua
I ka hānau ʻana o nā hōʻaliʻi.

Hānau ke kaikamahine hoʻonou o ka lani.
Hemo mai he keiki kāne,
ʻOʻili ka ua koko iluna.

Hānau ʻo Kū-walu me kāna kāne,
ʻO Kū-ihi-malanai-ākea.

Aʻai, e Pele, i kou ʻāina—
ʻĀina ka ʻōhiʻa, ka ulu hala i kai o Lele-iwi.

He moku Pana-ʻewa, he oka wale Kaʻū.

Text: N. B. Emerson, *Pele and Hiʻiaka*, pp. 122–124. Title
assigned.

He puʻu o Pele nui.
Kahi, e Pele, i kou ʻāina, hoʻolewa ke au.

ʻEliʻeli, kau mai.

II
Kū i Wai-lua ka pou hale a ka ipo.
Hoʻolono i ka uwalo, ka wawā nui
ʻO Ulupō ma oli nei; ʻaʻohe uwalo mai, e.
Aloha ʻino iā Ikuwa ma oli nei.
Ke lele la ka ʻeka mua,
Ka ʻino a ka makani.

Ukiuki, kolo e, kaulana,
Ka ua lele aku a lele mai,
Lele a Puhi-lala, lele a kaulana—
Ka hoaka, e Hiʻiaka, e!

Nō wai ke kānaenae?
Nō ka ʻohana a Haumea ke kānaenae.
Kuʻu ʻa e Kāne ke koʻa,
I ka ia nei manawa ia.
Nō Pele, nō Hiʻiaka nō ka honua,
Ka honua nei ka honua lewa,
Ka lani iluna.

O Ana-kū kū ka ʻaha iloko.
O Haʻamo he ala i hei ʻaʻe ʻia.

He pahu i kulaʻina, he pā i ʻaʻe ʻia.
He kahua i hele ʻia, he luana mauʻu,
He kaunana kō, ʻokana piko.

He hola moena, he lawena ipu kai.
He ukuhi ʻna wai, he kaumaha ʻai.
He haʻina nō ka hale, e.
Noa, noa ia hale—ua ʻaʻe ʻa,
Ua komohia nō waihona.

Kū ana o hālau olōlo,
Ka hale o Pele i noho ai.
Mākaʻikaʻi mai Kini o ke Akua.

Hoʻi aku e, hoʻi aku iwaho ʻna!
He kahuna pule ʻole, he ʻliʻi pule ʻole.
Mai komo wale mai i ka hale o Pele,
O koʻu Akua, la!

ʻEliʻeli, kau mai!

III

E kau ana kiko i ke alia kiko.
Hele a moʻa kiko ʻakāhi nei au.
Kāʻele puʻepuʻe, neʻineʻi,
Kāʻele pākikokiko.

Ua noa ka ʻāina, e kapu keiki,
E kapu ke nui, e kahe nā wai.
I ka hakē ana, kū ka ʻopeʻope.

O Kulipeʻe noho i ka Lua.
A lele, e, nā hōʻaliʻi o Kū-wawā.

O Kū-haili-moe, o ka nāʻele o Hawaiʻi,
ʻAkāhi nei au a hoʻi aku nei mai ou aku la,
A lele pakohana mai.

ʻEliʻeli, kau mai!

✿ ✿ ✿

Pele Raped

I

Dark clouds blasted, rain slashed
the face of the sky. Earth turned black
at the birth of princely children.

First a girl-child was born of the Goddess.
Then came the boy-child
and the blood-red rain poured down.

Then Kū-walu was born with a mate,
Malanai, the young tradewind.

And you, O Pele, ate of your land,
gorged on your groves of *'ōhi'a,*
your sacred fruiting pandanus
at Lele-iwi along the sea.

Pana-'ewa remained forested park,
Ka'ū became ashen wasteland.

By her labor Pele heaved into place a mountain.
Make and mar your land, Goddess Pele,
let your fire-streams flow!

O hovering powers, possess me—
help me in my telling!

II

So the lover lodges at Wai-lua with housepost erect.
Pele hears the call pounding out of Ulupō, beat of
    chanters,
but utters no answering cry,
ignores noise of singers in contest.
Yet love's first leap stirs the Goddess,
storm-thrust of that season
when the wind bows low over the land.

Gush of rain descends, angry tears,
rain-columns of weeping build and break,
fire spurts, flame springs, slackens, dies—
these symbols, O Hi'i-aka, must figure forth my tale.

For whom do I make this offering?
For the ancient seed of Haumea, her children and
    kin.
For them Kāne lowered down his coral reefs,
completed his work in Pele's time—
Pele's land, Hi'i-aka's land, bruised lands that
    shift, churn, slide.
The brooding earth drifts beneath the arch of the sky.

At Ana-kū the gods gathered.
The sacred road led through Ha'amo.
Now with drum dismantled drum song ends.
The wall's o'erleaped, the terrace trampled,
nothing remains save litter of straw,
trash of sugarcane, taro leavings,
heaps of odds and ends.

Spread mats and a clutter of dishes appears.
Here's much slopping of water, serving of food.
Yet the house rudely entered is a house of desecration.
Released from the kapu, what was sacred
is degraded, dust-trodden, the place of the kapu
    deflowered.

Where once rose Pele's temple
a common longhouse stands in a shambles,
troops of godlings stroll by on a visit.

Out! Out! Let the premises be cleansed!
Your priests are prayerless, words of your chiefs lack
    wings.
Enter not the house of Pele uninvited.
Come ye not without song, offering, prayer.

For Pele still lives, I swear as a fisherman,
and Pele is my god!

O hovering powers, possess me—
help me in my telling!

III

The kapu is broken, only boundary markers remain,
a few crossed ti-leaves, tattered streamers fluttering
    in the wind.
Men parcel out the marginal bounds of the patch.
Every watery ditch has been counted, each taro
    clump counted.

Let the land go free, children be cherished,
people secure, streams flow undisturbed. With the
    kapu broken
now let food bundles be plentiful in the field.

Kuli-pe'e-the-stumbler shall keep to her fiery Pit.
Clamorous chieftains have fled from their own
    hideous uproar.

Welcome, seed-bearing Kū-haili-moe,
soother of lands, planter of Hawaiʻi's forests and
 fields!
I go now in peace from your presence,
I who came in nakedness.

O hovering powers, possess me—
help me in my telling!

NOTES

I

birth of princely children: Narrative sequence in Oceanic
poetry frequently jumps about, ignoring straightforward
chronology. Thus the birth of Pele's children is men-
tioned before her actual seduction or rape, which is told
in the second section.

blood-red rain: This is given in the Hawaiian text as *uakoko,*
literally, 'blood rain'. Hawaiians used the expression to
refer to rainbow-colored mists and clouds, prismatic effects
seen in sun- and rain-filled valleys; also to distinguish a
heavy rain that turns streams rust-red from the wash of hill-
sides. All these associations are relevant, always with the
pervasive idea that rainbows and the color red, the blood
color, are manifestations of divinity.

Kū-walu: Literally, 'Kū [number] eight', or, as Emerson
puts it, "eighth in order of succession among Kū-gods."

Malanai: The name of Kū-walu's younger brother, Kū-
ʻihi-malanai-ākea, is obscure and may be an error in Emer-
son's text. If the name were simply Kū-ʻihi-malani-ākea,
it would translate as "sacred Kū in the spacious sky."

Lele-iwi: Name of cape along the Puna coast, near Hilo
and the Wai-luku river. The name also suggests "a grave-
yard, a scaffold, one perhaps on which the body (literally
the bones) of human sacrifices are left exposed" (Emer-
son, *Pele and Hiʻiaka*, p. 189).

II

Wai-lua: Probably the land division in Kaʻū, although
there is also a Wai-lua division in Hilo district.

Ulupō: Emerson was informed that the name referred to
a *heiau* at Kai-lua, Hawaiʻi. The term also means "dark,
dense growth," and suggests virility and sexual power.

storm-thrust: Emerson translates *ʻeka mua*, in the Hawaiian
text, as "the first blast of a storm; here used figuratively
to mean the first sexual ecstasy."

figure forth: This is given in the Hawaiian text as *hoaka*,
"a setting forth in figures," according to Emerson. The
term is rich in meanings suggesting revelation: "crescent-
shaped design at base of temple drum"; "shining, splen-
did"; "to cast a shadow"; "to open, as the mouth"; "spirit,
ghost."

seed of Haumea: Descendants of Haumea, goddess of child-
birth, mother of Pele and Hiʻi-aka and other members of
the fire family (*ʻohana*).

Ana-kū: According to Emerson, "name of a cave situ-
ated somewhere in the caldera of Kilauea, a place of as-
sembly for gods. Its use here is evidently for a highly
figurative purpose, and has, of course, to do with Pele and
her affair with Kama-puaʻa." In general, Emerson finds
a systematic sexual symbolism throughout the geographical
references in this part of the chant.

Haʻamo: Emerson's informant told him the term referred
to "the road to Ana-kū," presumably the passage to the
cave.

with drum dismantled: Emerson says that it is doubtful
whether the *pahu* of the Hawaiian text refers to a drum
or a post, but in any event the allusion is sexual and sym-
bolic: "In either case . . . the figure is designed to set
forth the confusion caused by the catastrophe—Pele's
debauchment."

III

Kuli-peʻe-the-stumbler: The name depicts Pele as an old
woman, crouching, crawling, stumbling across the country-
side—an allusion to the hitching, stumbling movement of
lava flows. The *Hawaiian Dictionary* gives for *kuli-peʻe*:
"to creep along as a sick person; to stumble awkwardly
along; to walk as though weak-kneed."

Kū-haili-moe: Same as Kū-moku-hāliʻi, a male fertility god
who adorns the islands with vegetation and figures in many
hula prayers. His special emblem is *lama*, various ebony
trees (*Diospyros*) endemic to Hawaiʻi. The wood was used
in medicine and displayed at the altar in Laka worship,
Laka being a kind of feminine symbol of sexual power
and enlightenment and a counterpart of Kū. Kū-moku-
hāliʻi, according to Martha Beckwith, appears prominently
in the Pele and Hiʻi-aka legends when Pele, jealous of Lohi-
ʻau's love for Hiʻi-aka, "invokes her gods, but they call
her unjust and blow away the flame [of Pele], for which
disloyalty she banishes them to the barren lands of Huli-
nuʻu; and that is how Kū-pulupulu, Kū-moku-hāliʻi, Kū-
ala-nawao, Kupa-ʻai-keʻe, and Kū-mauna came to sail away
and become canoe-makers in other lands" (*Hawaiian
Mythology*, pp. 176–177).

Ramble Round Hawai'i

THE CHANT WAS sometimes recited for its own sake, but it could also be performed as a string game. The various figures were manipulated so as to suggest a panorama of changing landscape as seen while traveling counter-clockwise from one to another of the six ancient districts of the island of Hawai'i.

🌺 🌺 🌺

He Huaka'i Ka'apuni ma Hawai'i

Kū e ho'opi'o ka lā
Ka lā i ke kula o Ahu-'ena
Komo i ka la'i o Kai-lua e—

'O Kona:
'O Kona ia i ke kai malino
Ke hele la i waho o Kapu-lau
Kani ka 'a'o i Wai-'ula'ula
A he alanui e waiho nei
A ke kanaka e hele ai la

Text: Mary Kawena Pukui. Title assigned.

'O Ka'ū:
'O Ka'ū ia, o Ka'ū kua makani
He ipu kai Pōhina nā ke A'e-loa
Lele koa'e i Kau-maea la e—

'O Puna:
'O Puna paia 'ala i ka hala
Kea'au 'ili'ili nehe 'ōlelo i ke kai
'O Puna ia la e—

'O Hilo:
'O Hilo ia o ka ua kinakinai
Ka ua mao 'ole o Hilo
He ua lū lehua ia nō Pana-'ewa e—

'O Hāmākua:
'O Hāmākua ia o ka pali Ko'olau
Ke ku'uku'u la i ke kaula
Ke 'aki la ka niho i ka ipu
I ka pali 'o Koholā-lele
'O Waipi'o, 'o Wai-manu e—

'O Kohala:
'O Kohala-iki, 'o Kohala-nui
'O Kohala-loko, 'o Kohala-waho
'O Pili, 'o Ka-lā-hiki-ola
Nā pu'u haele lua o Kohala

🏵 🏵 🏵

Ramble Round Hawai'i

The rising sun travels in an arc
reaches the flatlands of Ahu-'ena
enters Kai-lua's gentle landscape

This is Kona:
coastal Kona along the unruffled sea
where the sun rides ahead to Kapu-lau
where cry of the puffin-bird at Wai-'ula'ula
breaks the silence of the traveler's trail

And here's Ka'ū:
Ka'ū of the wind-swept back
where Pōhina's a pungent dish in the salty wind
while shining leapers at Kau-maea
soar like *koa'e*-birds through the air

And Puna:
where *hala*'s fragrance blows from Puna's branch-
    ing bowers
and pebbles at Kea'au whisper to the sea
Puna's forever there

With Hilo:
Hilo of perpetual rains
rains in a never-clearing gusty sky
scattering the fringed *lehua* of Pana-'ewa

And Hāmākua:
Hāmākua of the windward Ko'olau hills
where the traveler lowering himself by rope
grips the net of his carrying calabash between his teeth
descends the cliff at Koholā-lele
and those sheer-sided valleys Wai-pi'o and Wai-manu

Kohala last:
lesser Kohala, greater Kohala
inner Kohala, outer Kohala
and then Pili and Ka-lā-hiki-ola
companion hills traveling as a twain

NOTES

Ahu- 'ena: Originally a *heiau* (place of worship) for
human sacrifices at Kai-lua, Hawai'i. It was restored by
Ka-mehameha I. Literally, 'red-hot heap'.

This is Kona: The leeward district, Kona was noted for
its prosperous, almost motionless fishing waters, restful
ways, silent beaches, and deserted coastal trails.

And here's Ka'ū: A desert district with the poetic name
kua makani, 'windy back'. Strong winds blow at Pōhina, a
cliff near Honu-'apo dampened by salty sea sprays—"like
a meat dish" (*he ipukai*).

Kau-maea: At Kau-maea, inland from Pai-a-ha'a, there
was a dusty mound and pit for holding leaping contests,
in which the athletes resembled the flying tropicbird, the

koa'e. After the sport the sweaty men would wipe themselves with fern leaves (hence the name Kau-maea [Kau-maea-lele-kawa 'place stench leaping place']), before walking a mile or so to Pai-a-ha'a for a freshening dip and surfing.

And Puna: Famous for its fragrant pandanus (*hala*) trees, whose scent was wafted by the sea breezes. Puna people liked to tuck bracts of the pandanus behind thatching sticks, also to sprinkle them under mats.

With Hilo: Not the town only but the entire district, associated with abundant rains and especially with the far-blown red *lehua* of the *'ōhi'a* forests, symbolic of sexual allure, also of a sweetheart, beloved friend or relative.

And Hāmākua: A windward district of towering coastal cliffs, waterfalls, and almost inaccessible valleys opening on the sea.

Kohala last: The district included shoreland, an extinct volcano, a mountainous upland famous for its strong dry wind, 'Apa'apa'a.

Ka-lā-hiki-ola: The hill named Ka-lā-hiki-ola, 'the life-bringing sun', gave its name to the surrounding area.

Behold

THE CHANT IS traditional in theme and structure. It is organized around four words, four indispensable terms in speaking Hawaiian, the directional words *luna* 'above'; *lalo* 'below'; *mauka* 'inland', 'mountainward'; *makai* 'toward the sea'. School children in Hawai'i sometimes learn this perfect chant in kindergarten, in the original; and it is taught in park recreational programs. In compact form, with its generous, simple, strong rhythms and gestures, the chant demonstrates the Polynesian sense of the kinship of man and nature, the continuity of life in space, the magic of language, and the power of the poet's creations to triumph over time:

> ... to forge links between past, present and future, and "tread" natural and supernatural regions to define their qualities and to name their occupants and localities. (Luomala, *Voices on the Wind*, p. 67)

❀ ❀ ❀

E 'Ike Mai

I luna la, i luna
Nā manu o ka lewa

I lalo la, i lalo
Nā pua o ka honua

I uka la, i uka
Nā ulu lāʻau

I kai la, i kai
Nā iʻa o ka moana

Haʻina mai ka puana
A he nani ke ao nei

❀ ❀ ❀

Behold

Above, above
all birds in air

below, below
all earth's flowers

    Text: Mary Kawena Pukui. Title assigned.

inland, inland
all forest trees

seaward, seaward
all ocean fish

sing out and say
again the refrain

Behold this lovely world

Appendix:
Class and Commentary

HAWAIIAN CHANTED POETRY of the nineteenth century was a continuation and development of ancient oral traditions and practices, with deep roots in religion, ceremony, social custom, and linguistic expression and behavior. In earlier commentary we have paid relatively little attention to the important subject of poetic performance, spoken or chanted, and as sometimes accompanied by dance. The following notes are not at all intended, however, as a comprehensive discussion of the twenty-nine texts in their performance aspect. Indeed, most of these afterthoughts and suggestions may be regarded simply as remnants, chips from the workshop, left over from our collaborations, scattered readings, and long discussions.

For a full and very authoritative analysis of Hawaiian poetry and song of the nineteenth century, especially as it reflects the structure of the Hawaiian language and earlier traditions and styles, the reader should consult the valuable collection of Hawaiian songs translated and edited by Samuel H. Elbert and Noelani Mahoe, *Nā Mele o Hawai'i Nei: 101 Hawaiian Songs* (Honolulu: University of Hawaii Press, 1970).

SHARK HULA FOR KA-LANI-ʻŌPUʻU

A shark hula (*hula manō*), as noted in the *Hawaiian Dictionary*, was a "sitting dance imitative of sharks." Emerson places the shark hula, along with the *hula kōlea* (plover), the *hula ʻīlio* (dog), and *hula puaʻa* (pig), as "one of the animal dances." He also says that "the last and only mention of its performance in modern times was in the year 1847, during the tour ... which Kamehameha III made about Oahu" (*Unwritten Literature*, p. 221).

It is doubtful whether Emerson himself was aware of the existence of the *Shark Hula for Ka-lani-ʻōpuʻu*, for if he had known it he would surely have found a place in his survey for so distinguished an example of the traditional and more archaic poetry of the Hawaiians. Mrs. Pukui considers the *Shark Hula for Ka-lani-ʻōpuʻu* as an example of the type of hula that could be "for dancing and not for dancing." The text of the chant states: "Ka-lani-ʻōpuʻu ... this is your name chant [*O kou inoa ia*]." Perhaps a fuller classification would describe the composition as, first, a name chant honoring Ka-lani-ʻōpuʻu's ancestral line and *ʻaumākua*, and then as a chant that was sometimes but not invariably performed as a sitting hula with totemic movements and gestures. The chanting style suitable for such a name chant would have depended partly on the occasion and partly on the capacity and skill of the chanter, and could have been either the *kepakepa*

rhythmic style, clear, fairly rapid, and not requir-
ing great reserves of breath, or else in the more in-
spired *ho'ae'āe* style, involving prolonging the
vowels and sometimes adding other complex tonal
effects.

There is reason to believe that the *Shark Hula for
Ka-lani-'ōpu'u* must have been exactly the type of
sacred hula in the resounding tones—"hideous
noises at night"—of which early missionaries be-
lieved they recognized paganism in one of its most
nerve-racking forms. Though the text of the chant
has survived in oral tradition long enough to be
recorded in writing, it is doubtful whether many
full-scale performances of it occurred after the
great religious awakening of the late 1830s and the
establishment of the "government of learning" un-
der Ka-mehameha III. Helen Roberts, in her *Ancient
Hawaiian Music*, reported that the only mention
of a performance of the *hula manō* she could find
in modern times "was in 1847 on the island of
Oahu, in the 'lonely and romantic valley of Waimea'
during a tour made by Kamehameha III. No trace
of it was found in the recent survey [1923–1924]"
(p. 169).

CHANT OF WELCOME FOR KA-MEHAMEHA
The chant could be labeled a song for a chief
(*mele ali'i*), but it is also an example of a *kāhea*,
a call or greeting. Various kinds of greetings—wel-

comes, prayers for admittance, responses, and so forth—played an important part in old Hawaiian life at all levels. A *kāhea ʻai*, for example, was "a call to come and eat; a prayer calling on the gods to share the food."

Ululani's welcome of Ka-mehameha implies that he will be received not merely as the conqueror but also as the life-bringer and companion of gods. The style of such a greeting, whether in the *kepakepa* manner or with drawn-out vowels—*E ko----mo!*— would seek to express the spontaneity of the chiefess' aloha for the godlike man as well as her respect for the warrior.

BIRTH CHANT FOR KAU-I-KE-AO-ULI

A birth chant (*mele hānau*) is similar to a name chant. Both concern the origins and ancestry of a line of ruling chiefs. The main difference is that the birth chant, as the term suggests, concentrates at some point on the circumstances—cosmological, astrological, and by necessity gynecological—of the actual begetting and bearing of the infant.

Helen H. Roberts, *Ancient Hawaiian Music,* quotes extensively from the Hawaiian historian Samuel M. Kamakau on the subject of *koʻihonua,* genealogical history:

> The composing of meles was a special education in those old days and certain people became very famous

for their achievements along this line. The recital of
some of these meles, such as the *ko'ihonua*, or genea-
logical history, was somewhat different from other
recitals, in that the tone was almost of one note, in
order that the words could be distinctly heard and un-
derstood; the voice was held in the throat so that it
would not be harsh. A *ko'ihonua* mele is one which
relates to the forefathers of the Hawaiian people and
to the history of the kings and their accomplishments
together with the deeds of their ancestors. In the *ko-
'ihonua* mele of Kuali'i, the Kumuali'i and the Kumu-
lipo were preserved, and in the mele of Peleiholani, the
genealogical tree of Ololo and Haloa was given, and in
the mele of Kamahanao, the history of Palikū and
Punaimua were made known.

In these compositions great care was taken in order
to have the details accurate and the names correct,
and this is the reason for the great value of these ge-
nealogical histories of the ancestors of the Hawaiians to-
day. These genealogical trees go further back than the
time of Wakea who is commonly known as the forefather
of the Hawaiian people. . . .

In the *olioli* or hymnal meles there is the underlying
purpose of worship. The tone of the voice is different
from that used for the other meles, being lighter, al-
though held very low in the throat. The sound issues
gurgling, the breath is held for a very long time and
as the words come out as though falling from the tip of
the tongue the mouth is opened only slightly and no
heavy veins are to be seen along the neck. When one
can do this in the manner described he is considered
an expert.

The composing of the *ko'ihonua, ha'ikupuna* [relating

one's ancestors] and *kamakua* [telling of one's par-
ents] meles was conducted under very strict tabu and only
by those who were well versed in the history of the
time. The tabu placed on the spots where these meles
were composed was no less than that employed at the com-
posing of a genealogical history. Meles foretelling the
future and those for worship were generally composed
when the spirit moved the prophet. Meles in honor of
persons, for the glorification of the king, for thankful-
ness or for expressing lamentation and various other
kinds, were often made by a single individual and were
completed in a short time, but on the other hand, if a
mele was to be composed to reveal that a given individ-
ual was stingy, good, bad, brave, and so on, then two or
more persons together composed the mele. In large com-
positions the composer generally had several persons
with him and to each a line was assigned, and sometimes
two, and as each line was completed the composer des-
ignated one person who took that line and studied it,
committing it to memory. In this manner several lines
were composed at one sitting and when completed they
were recited by the different ones. Then the others took
them and in a short time the whole mele was learned by
heart. Should the mele be short, one or two could sit and
compose it.... (pp. 59–60)

Roberts points out in *Ancient Hawaiian Music* that
there is "some difference of opinion whether the
word *ko'ihonua* refers to a genealogical chant or
to the method of chanting." In answer to the question
she quotes N. B. Emerson, editor of David Malo's
Hawaiian Antiquities, as follows:

Haku mele, literally to weave a song. A mele for the glorification of a king, born or still unborn, was called a *mele inoa*. This was a eulogy or panegyric of the ancestral virtues, real or fictitious, of a king or princeling. . . . *Ko-i-honua* was not, as mistakenly supposed, a particular kind of mele. It related to the tone or manner of utterance of the *mele inoa*; it meant that the *inoa* was to be recited in an ordinary conversational tone, and not after the manner called *oli*. That is applied to a singing tone. The *ko-i-honua* manner of reciting a *mele inoa* made it more intelligible and therefore more acceptable to the king. . . . (p. 60)

Roberts adds some useful comment distinguishing between the *oli* and *kepakepa* styles in the performance of genealogical chants.

This same kind of conversational chanting is also known as *kepakepa*, which, as illustrated to me by a man who once held the position of reviser of meles in the reign of King Kalakaua, was merely a rather rapid and expressionless reciting of the syllables, in what might be written as sixteenth notes, without regard to accent and with no variation in length.

As Kamakau has it, the meles recited in olioli fashion were primarily religious chants. At the present time, whatever may have obtained in the past, although prayers and any kind of religious chants are recited in olioli fashion, others [of secular type] are also given in this manner. (p. 60–61)

Emerson has stated that name chants and birth chants were sometimes the result of group composition, as when different genealogical experts might be summoned by a chief to help compose a chant, or when several members of a family would each contribute a particular share—his or her *kuleana*—to the total work. Such appears to have been the method of composition followed in the *Birth Chant for Kau-i-ke-ao-uli*. Mrs. Pukui's typed manuscript of the text of the chant, among her personal archives, names authors who contributed the first five sections: I, by Liholiho (produced when he was a boy of fourteen or fifteen); II, by 'Au'au; III, by Hauna; IV, by Pi'opi'o; V, by Hehena.

The opening lines of this sacred chant describe the pangs of the mother, the high chiefess Ke-ōpū-o-lani, already mother of the young Liholiho. It is important to realize that the rank of Ke-ōpū-o-lani was even loftier than that of Ka-mehameha I. According to Kamakau, Ke-ōpū-o-lani "was of so high a tabu that he [Ka-mehameha] had to take off his *malo* [loincloth] before he came into her presence, but he desired above everything to have children of the highest rank.... Those of his children whom Kamehameha considered in the line of succession he always treated as though they were his gods" (*Ruling Chiefs*, p. 208).

The remaining sections of the chant identify the birth of the young chief with the processes of nature divinely empowered: the creation of the earth, night, the island of Hawai'i, and so forth. A sexual dualism

underlies the symbolic fabric of the chant. Cosmic
events become personified and mythologically de-
fined in the naming of the first ancestors, Wākea
(Kea) and Papa, and the allusions to their mating.
The mysterious reiterated questions and set responses
—"Now a chief shall be above. / Who shall be be-
low?"—exemplify the Polynesian dualistic con-
ception, in some contexts, of "higher" and "lower"
aspects of the physical environment and also of a
superior and inferior sex. Despite her divine rank,
as a woman Ke-ōpū-o-lani is still as such inferior
to the divine man.

> The male was superior and hence *kapu* [according to the
> anthropologist E. S. C. Handy], embodying the divine
> aspects manifest in the sky (*lani*), the higher gods
> (*akua*), in light (*ao*), and life (*ola*). On the other
> hand the female was common (*noa*), related to earth
> (*papa*) and darkness (*pō*), which harbored corrup-
> tion (*haumia*).... Manhood was, therefore, constantly
> shielded by *kapu* of sanctity; while woman was period-
> ically subject to *kapu* of defilement. (*Cultural Revolu-
> tion*, p. 8)

Though female divinity was identified with earth
and male with the sky, there seems to have been no
rigid "superordinate-subordinate relationship"
between classes of creatures and classification sys-
tems in ancient Hawaiian belief. The Hawaiian con-
ception of the natural world, according to Laura
Thompson,

. . . is extraspatial in terms of the western concept of
absolute space. There is a spatial dimension expressed,
however, if we think of the domain of the sea as com-
pletely surrounding that of land—on the oceanic islands
of the Pacific. And the natural time dimension is ex-
pressed, of course, in the Hawaiian genealogical se-
quences. (*Secret of Culture*, p. 82)

Linguistic devices of repetition, naming, parallel-
ism, phonetic patterning, and a pervasive element
of monotony are characteristic of the language of
magical rituals everywhere in the world. The aes-
thetics of this kind of esoteric poetry, akin to rites
of healing, and serving as a medium for expressing
mysteries, enacting sacraments, and linking human
beings and historic circumstances to cosmic and
supernatural events, have been studied recently by
Jerome Rothenberg, in a work appropriately en-
titled *Technicians of the Sacred*:

What's of interest here isn't the matter of the myth but
the power of repetition and naming (monotony, too) to
establish the presence of a situation-in-its-entirety. This
involves the acceptance (by poets and hearers) of an
indefinite extension of narrative time and the belief
that language (i.e., poetry) can make-things-present
by naming them. (p. 385)

THE OLD WAY AND THE NEW

The texts are quotations from Kamakau's news-
paper writings, published originally during the

early 1870s, and he does not indicate their pro-
venience. The first excerpt, from a pre-Christian
chant (*The Sea of Wai-a-lua*), was obviously chosen
by Kamakau to illustrate the fusion of religious
myth and heroic tradition to be found in the old
poetry, and its elaborately controlled sound tex-
ture. The second quotation (*The Lord of Eternal
Life*) exemplifies a style that, after the coming of
the missionaries in the 1820s and 1830s, developed
throughout the rest of the century among Hawaiians
who were Christians, often profoundly devout, and
who felt moved to utter their new-found faith in the
old language and cadences. The second excerpt may
be described as an example of this new style based
on *Hōʻike ʻAna* (Revelation). Hawaiian converts
associated the idea of Christian Revelation with
a quarterly magazine for Sunday school use, en-
titled *Hoʻike*, established by the early Congrega-
tionalist missionary Hiram Bingham. Apparently
the form *hōʻike* came to be commonly used to de-
scribe any poetical composition based on scriptural
matter.

One formal feature of *The Lord of Eternal Life* Ka-
makau failed to mention: it is quite untraditional in
its use of a regular sequence of rhymes.

A SURFING SONG
As the earlier introductory comment has indicated,
the text is an adaptation, dating back to the Ka-lā-

kaua period, of *A Name Chant for Naihe*, com-
posed originally in the 1820s by the personal chanter
of a chief of Kona named Naihe, who was a noted
athlete and orator. Ben Finney, in his *Surfing: The
Sport of Hawaiian Kings*, tells us that "often a surf-
riding chief had a personal surf chant that pro-
claimed his glory and skill. To deliver it there had
to be a chanter whom every chief kept in his retinue"
(p. 45). Not a great many texts of such traditional
surf chants seem to have survived, although there
are numerous references in Hawaiian legends and in
accounts of early voyagers to the important place
occupied by surfing in old-time Hawaiian life,
among commoners as well as the *ali'i* class, and
among women as well as men. One of the most
complete and authentic examples known today of
the surf chant is Mrs. Pukui's *A Name Chant for
Naihe*, quoted briefly by Finney, and more ex-
tensively by Mrs. Pukui in her "Songs (meles) of
old Ka'u, Hawaii" (*Journal of American Folklore*,
vol. 62, no. 245, pp. 247–258). The Bishop Museum
has a tape recording of the full *A Name Chant for
Naihe*, the source of the excerpts quoted by Mrs.
Pukui in her article and Finney in his book on surfing.

FOREST CHANT IN PRAISE OF LAKA

Emerson describes the *Forest Chant in Praise of
Laka* as an "adulatory prayer (*Kānaenae*) in
adoration of Laka," and elsewhere defines *kānaenae*

as "a propitiatory sacrifice; an intercession; a part
of a prayer" (*Unwritten Literature*, pp. 16, 267).
No dancing was involved. The sacrificial feature,
requiring the killing of a wild pig, in very early
times must have been prominent in the ritual im-
plied in the present text. The *Hawaiian Dictionary*
gives a much more detailed definition of *kānaenae*
than that found in Emerson's survey, together with
valuable comment on performing style: "Chanted
supplicating prayer; chant of eulogy (the chanter
hesitates at regular intervals to recover breath); tone
variation is greater and pitch may be higher than
in the *olioli*); to pray thus; to sacrifice."

SONGS FROM "PELE AND HI'I-AKA"
The hundreds and hundreds of surviving chants,
dance-songs, prayers, charms, and incantations
introduced by native storytellers and composers in
the Pele and Hi'i-aka cycle lie scattered through
the Hawaiian-language newspapers, with their dates
of publication ranging all the way from the 1860s
to the 1920s. A valuable compilation and redaction
of the legends in translation, focusing on the tri-
angular love story of Pele and Hi'i-aka and the
handsome chief of Kaua'i, Lohi'au, was published
in 1915 by Nathaniel B. Emerson, translator and
editor, but has long been out of print. A compara-
tive general analysis of some major Pele texts and
documents is included by Martha Beckwith in her

Hawaiian Mythology, first published in 1940. The best introduction to the Pele-Hiʻi-aka cycle as a classic of the Polynesian imagination is Katharine Luomala's *Voices on the Wind: Polynesian Myths and Chants*, especially chapter two, "Within the Circle of the Sea."

The six chants presented here give no idea whatever of the range and variety of chant- or song-types found in the cycle as a whole. An intensive analysis of the materials must be left to future scholarship.

Musicologists and other experts with a knowledge of ancient Hawaiian oral poetry, music, and dance distinguish between two main types of Hawaiian poems: those not for dancing, called *oli*, and those accompanied by dancing, *hula*. Some poems, however, could be recited either in *oli* or *hula* style. The *oli* class furthermore provided alternate styles of recitation: *kepakepa*, a rhythmical, conversational style, aimed especially at clear enunciation; *hoʻāe-ʻāe*, distinguished by short phrases and prolonged vowels, sometimes interspersed with a fluctuating trill; and some authorities mention also the *ʻai haʻa* style, an exaggeration apparently of the *hoʻāeʻāe*, marked by the use of strained, guttural tones, providing effects of intensity verging on the bombastic. In the chanting of love poems, the *hoʻāeʻāe* style was frequently used to express moods of tenderness,

while the *'ai ha'a* was regarded especially appro-
priate for the more impassioned expression of love.
In any event, it is probably true that the nature
of the occasion often determined the style of per-
formance, and that individual dancers of marked
originality developed personal styles or what to-
day would be called individual interpretations.

The hula chants as rendered in performance are
sometimes not easy to distinguish solely by ear from
oli recitations. However, as might be expected, hula
chants by and large have strong rhythmic swing, and
for the most part hold to duple time. Dorothy M.
Kahananui points out that hula chants are more
melodic than the *oli* type, which keeps to a limited
tonal range (*Music of Hawaii*, p. 17). Another dif-
ference is that the hula chant is less likely to favor
a principal or "general level" tone.

The name of the hero of the Pele-Hi'i-aka cycle,
Lohi'au (Lohi-'au), is usually spelled today with
the glottal stop. One oral tradition, based on lin-
guistic evidence, holds that the name means "slow,
tardy, taking a long time," and thus strikes a note
of humor when applied to the lover-hero. Though
this interpretation of the name is well established,
it is by no means certain. Emerson, who spells
the word as "Lohiau," was either unaware of the
humorous interpretation or chose to ignore it as
problematic.

LEI CHANT FOR QUEEN EMMA

The chant was performed in the dignified *oli* style.

The introductory note pointed out the relationship of the lei-giving ceremony to the custom of *ho'okupu,* the presentation of material tribute and gifts to a ruling chief. The term *ho'okupu* itself means "to cause growth," and the annual *makahiki* agricultural festival might be described as having been a sort of huge *ho'okupu* intended to celebrate fertility, and of course to honor the ruling chief. Perhaps what should be emphasized here is an important difference between *ho'okupu* as an economic institution and lei-giving as a less utilitarian and more aesthetic rite. Flower leis presented solely as emblems of beauty and love were without exchange value, unlike bananas, chickens, and pigs; in short, they were without any consumptive use, except to be worn and displayed. The presentation of flower leis thus provided an occasion for ritualized offerings of symbolic aloha, and this was at the same time a genuine social value though it had no obvious or immediate economic purpose.

Nevertheless, an essential aspect of the symbolic lei-giving ceremony, like the *ho'okupu* in its primitive form, was its ancient alliance with fertility rites and with the legends that developed with them and perhaps sometimes out of them. One of the first occupations of the Pele sisters on arriving at their home in the Hawaiian Islands was to busy them-

selves with making leis of the wild flowers they
found on the various islands. Later, toward the close
of the Pele and Hi'i-aka romance, when Hi'i-aka
finds herself alone with Lohi'au on the brink of
Kīlauea crater, she weaves three *lehua* leis. Two of
these she winds round the neck of Lohi'au; she
adorns herself with the third. While she is stringing
her leis she sings:

> The *wahine* Hi'iaka
> gathered the flowers,
> pierced them, strung them with her hands.
> Four strands of *lehua* are bound within the lei
> of the *wahine*, which means that now she's yours . . .
> (Retranslated from the original in Emerson, *Pele and
> Hi'iaka*, p. 191).

At the close of the song, the girl-woman-wife first
places her arms around the willing Lohi'au's neck
and then embraces him more completely.

The symbolic implications of the lei-giving cere-
mony are naturally erotic, but within their total
span they are generous and inclusive. In their larger
range they may encompass the feelings that bind
members of a family to each other, parents with
their children, friend with friend, islander with
islander and, in traditional Hawai'i, native with
stranger.

SONG OF THE WORKERS ON HOWLAND ISLAND

Pua-ka-ʻilima, as Hawaiians like to call it, is a
song for dancing, traditionally performed as a
hula pā ipu, also called the *kuolo,* a dance accom-
panied by the gourd drum. Emerson, *Unwritten
Literature,* describes the *hula pā ipu* as "a hula of
dignified character, in which all the performers
maintained the kneeling position and accompanied
the songs with the solemn tones of the *ipu,* with which
each one was provided" (p. 73). He goes on to
differentiate between the *hula pā ipu* and the *hula
ālaʻapapa,* the latter being the most elevated type
of hula employed in ancient times for a sacred or
religious performance. Its style was stately, formal,
sacerdotal, at the same time very strong in dramatic
suggestion. It was limited to only moderate physical
actions. The *hula pā ipu,* less restrained and stylized,
was at times "marked with great vigor and demon-
strativeness, so that in moments of excitement
and for the expression of passion, fierce joy, or
grief the *ipu* might be lifted on high and wildly
brandished."

Emerson's examples of *mele* used for the *hula pā
ipu* are chiefly chosen from "the archaic period,
which closed in the early part of the eighteenth
century." Several of the Emerson texts concern
love adventures—"the soliloquy of a lover es-
tranged from his mistress" (p. 83), a "passionate
episode in the life of a lover, looked at from the

standpoint of old age" (pp. 78–79), a *mele* symbolizing "the flight of a man in his deep-laden pirogue, abducting the woman of his love" (p. 77). Queen Emma's charming *Pua-ka-'ilima* in translation seems a fairly sedate example of the *hula pā ipu* when compared with Emerson's in the more ancient vein, but readers should allow for the animation and vigor of this dance-song for males as it was no doubt first performed by the Hawaiian guano diggers on their wind-blasted mid-Pacific isle.

Lady Franklin, visiting South Point on Hawai'i in the year 1861, has described in her unpublished journal the dance of a Hawaiian youth who entertained his companions on a gourd calabash. It is easy to imagine the crew on Howland Island dancing with the same gusto as that displayed by Lady Franklin's Naki, a young servant in a scarlet shirt, who on Sabbath morning began "a dancing or drinking song addressed to or sung by one of their old gods," and, surrounded by his appreciative audience, "squatted on ground with drinking calabash, which he patted and dandled like a baby, stretched out arms and other antics. I was rather vexed and told Mr. Kalakaua [I] thought it best come to an end." (Korn, *Victorian Visitors*, pp. 42–43)

ERRAND

Modern in atmosphere, this *oli* chant neverthe-less derives from ancient tradition, the composition in praise of a chief (*mele aliʻi*). Under a chief's righteous protection, such as that of Ka-mehameha V for his workers on Molokaʻi, his people might well express their aloha in a chant of gratitude (*mele māhalo*).

Though traditional in type, the individual style suggests the work of a literate mid-nineteenth-century Hawaiian Christian, a practiced composer aware of an audience also literate in the Hawaiian language and Bible, and yet respectful of *kahuna* wisdom, especially when it is accompanied by skill in herb medicine and concern for the people's health and well-being. The composer moves easily and with dignity among the diverse elements of his world—steam transportation, modern methods of labor, deeds of chiefly magnanimity, Christian compassion expressed in Biblical metaphor—all harmoniously ordered in his praise of Ka-mehameha V.

MR. THURSTON'S WATER-DRINKING BRIGADE

The Hawaiian term *mele inu wai*, 'water-drinking song', came into use in the nineteenth century for Western-style songs sung—and sometimes com-posed—by members of a temperance union, usually shepherded by a missionary or a layman of repute. In this specimen, only the landscape and topog-

raphy, the perennial seashore to mountain orien-
tation, link the chant with poetic conventions of the
past. Though the verses lent themselves to choral
performance, they were also very well suited for
publication in the columns of one of the weekly
Hawaiian-language newspapers. The editors were
hospitable to compositions reflecting the interests
of their readership, and the moral tone of the *mele*
could not but bring encouragement and renewed
dedication to their missionary friends.

ALAS FOR EVE

The *mele* may be placed in the *Hō'ike 'Ana*
(Revelation) class, because of the Scriptural deriva-
tion of its matter. The four-line stanzaic form is
typical of the Hawaiianized hymn (*hīmeni*), which
was sometimes chanted but gradually, as the Ha-
waiians developed an ear for Western melody and
scale, came to be sung to Christian religious airs.
Eventually the term *hīmeni* was extended to cover
any tune or song not used for hulas. *Alas for Eve*
does not appear in standard Hawaiian hymnals and
its air seems to have disappeared.

THE PRINCE'S WORDS TO THE PRINCESS

According to Emerson, the *mele* belonged to
the class of the *hula 'ulī'ulī*, socalled from the
rattle that accompanied the dance. The rattle was
made of a small gourd about the size of a large
orange filled with enough seeds (sometimes canna

seeds) so as to make a pronounced rustling sound when shaken—a sustained "whoosh" not unlike the sound of the surf on certain beaches. The gourd could be shaken by one hand against the palm of the other or it could be dropped to the thigh—"or making excursions in one direction and another." The performers were usually the older, less agile women (*ho‘opa‘a*) who manipulated the rattles while squatting. "In some performances of this hula which the author has witnessed," Emerson tells us, "the *‘ōlapa* [dancer as distinct from chanter] also took part, in one case a woman who stood and cantillated the song with movement and gesture while the *ho‘opa‘a* devoted themselves exclusively to handling the *‘ulī‘ulī* rattles" (*Unwritten Literature*, p. 107).

Emerson describes the *hula ‘ulī‘ulī* as lacking in the dignity and elevation of the *hula āla‘apapa* (reciting with dramatic mime, in the archaic style, heroic episodes of the past), the *hula pā ipu* (gourd drum dance), and the *hula Pele* (concerned with Pele legends). Helen Roberts, in her *Ancient Hawaiian Music*, makes no such distinction, but confines her remarks chiefly to musical analysis of the tonal and rhythmic qualities of the *‘ulī‘ulī* chants. Her illustrations include certain chants that in subject matter are highly dignified—for example, a name chant for Ka-pi‘o-lani—although not in the dramatic style of the ancient *hula āla‘apapa*.

The present version in English is not in any degree faithful to the text as a chant for *'ulī'ulī* performance. However, as a free adaptation that assists in comprehending the "story," perhaps this experimental rendering has possibilities as a libretto for a Victorian-Hawaiian ballet, a workshop experiment in dance, music, and theater.

A shorter version of the *mele* has been published, under the title *Alekōki*, in *Nā Mele o Hawai'i Nei*, p. 32.

FOREST TREES OF THE SEA

The *mele* is an example of the *ho'oipoipo*, "wooing song," "love song," "sweetheart song." It is an unusually fine example of the class that flourished best throughout the nineteenth century, especially when sung to an air. In *Forest Trees of the Sea* the composer succeeds in blending the symbolism of antiquity—the allusion to Māmala and the restless sea—with contemporary experience. The note of modernity is sounded in the memorable image of the tall-masted whalers of Honolulu and Marblehead and Gloucester. The modernity is reinforced by the richly projected sense of psychological urgency, the singer's need for her lover. Although we cannot know for certain, we may imagine that the lover is a foreigner and not Hawaiian.

Despite the modernity of its subject, *Forest Trees of the Sea* was sung in a traditional Hawaiian style, untouched by Western influence.

PIANO AT EVENING

Piano at Evening was composed as a *mele hula,*
a dance-song, performed with bamboo rattles. How-
ever, because of the modernity of the experience
evoked, the singer's discovery of beauty and fasci-
nation in a piano and a mirror, the *mele* does not fit
easily into traditional classifications. Yet it has the
spontaneity and lyric rightness of certain ancient
songs found in the Pele and Hi'i-aka cycle, in which
a singer addresses the object that has cast its spell
over his imagination.

Pālea, the composer, a resident of Ka'ū, was
steeped in the traditional lore and the poetry of
the region. He was a namesake, says Mrs. Pukui,
who knew his family as near neighbors, of a certain
Pālea who was among the natives on shore when
Captain Cook anchored off Ke-ala-ke-kua Bay.

A photograph of Kulu-wai-maka, Pālea's younger
brother, appearing to be a man in his late eighties,
was published in *Paradise of the Pacific,* April 1942.
A dignified figure with a crown of long white hair,
Kulu-wai-maka is shown wearing the tapa cloth robes
in which during the 1930s he recited chants at Lā-
lani Village in Wai-kīkī.

BILL THE ICE SKATER

The verses were composed by a literate Hawaiian
who could depend on the sense of humor of his au-
dience and its capacity to be amused by Bill's bi-

lingual struggle to boast about his success as an ice
skater—"*Mi no hau.*" The tradition behind the
poem is not any *mele* or literary type so much as it
is simply a cultural trait of Hawaiians, their ability
to find amusement and subject for laughter in them-
selves, as in all persons who must struggle to learn
a new language, play a new role, master a new set
of tricks. According to Mrs. Pukui, *Bill the Ice
Skater* was performed originally by a Mormon at
a show to raise money for the Mormon Church. The
air, if the verses had one, has disappeared.

WHAT IS A BOY LIKE?

Introductory comment has indicated that the
verses are thoroughly untraditional. They are signed
"Hawaii," and were obviously intended to enter-
tain a newspaper-reading audience. The images
include a mixture of animate and inanimate objects,
some of which like the horse and sheep (but certainly
not the *dia*) had been introduced into Hawai'i as
early as the 1790s, along with articles of com-
merce—the mirror and the cart wheel—that must
have followed not long after. There are numerous
references to specifically Hawaiian sights and
sounds, but these are only generalized and are not
very sharply communicated—volcanic steam, a
roaring sea, and the sound of the '*ūkēkē.*

Although repetition and parallel structure are
common features of Hawaiian rhetoric, here the

pattern seems insistently rigid and mechanical, aimed rather at the inward eye than toward the listening ear and the felt world of immediate experience. One is tempted to find the model for these engaging verses in a children's picture book, perhaps a first-grade reader, with illustrations of the subject—the red flower, the sling, the rebellious soldier—accompanied by the appropriate caption in the margin or on the opposite printed page.

ALL THE FOLKS AT ʻULA-KŌHEO

The verses could have been a direct contribution to a Hawaiian newspaper; or perhaps a pleased recipient passed the greeting (*kāhea*) along to the paper's editor for publication. The literate author takes pleasure in his memories and his Hawaiian origins, obviously enjoying his foreign adventures all the more when they entail the discovery of a home away from home.

SURE A POOR MAN

The song could be recited in the *kepakepa* rhythmic and conversational style as well as sung to the tune of *When Johnny Comes Marching Home*. Nineteenth-century Hawaiians would have assigned the *mele* to the general class of *hīmeni*, not for dancing and on any modern topic.

SONG OF THE CHANTER KA-ʻEHU

Earlier commentary has mentioned Ka-ʻehu's originality. This *mele* might be described as an unusual combination of two classes of traditional chants: the *mele nemanema,* the chant of criticism, and the *mele hoʻowēuwē,* a chant of lamentation. However, in the end, this last of Ka-ʻehu's chants eludes facile classification, even though it sometimes employs such traditional formulas as the references to tears and to the last glimpse of the homeland.

THE LOVE OF GOD

Like *Alas for Eve,* the verses are an example of *Hōʻike ʻAna* (Revelation), in the form of a *hīmeni,* for singing to an air. The song does not appear in any of the standard Hawaiian hymnals.

FIRE CHANT FOR KING KA-LĀ-KAUA

Broadly speaking, the chant is an example of a *mele aliʻi,* a song honoring a chief; more specifically it is an *inoa ahi,* a "fire-name [chant]," celebrating Ka-lā-kaua's descent and his right to the fire-burning kapu. As indicated earlier, the chant was composed for newspaper publication and was printed in *Nuhou (The News),* a journalistic enterprise of Walter Murray Gibson. *Nuhou* supported "Hawaiʻi for the Hawaiians," a strong monarchic

system, and a Hawaiian Kingdom more conscious
of its historical and cultural affinities with Poly-
nesians everywhere, the people of Oceania, and
particularly the people of Southeast Asia.

Undoubtedly the chant was performed on various
occasions years after its composition, almost cer-
tainly when 'Io-lani Palace was dedicated in 1879
and probably later at the time of Ka-lā-kaua's coro-
nation in 1883. As a type of name chant, it could be
recited either in the *oli* manner with elongated
vowels or in the plainer but markedly rhythmic
manner of *kepakepa*.

THE PEARL

The chant, in the dignified *oli* style, illustrates
some of the features of royal addresses and proc-
lamations, as this type of rhetoric had developed
in Hawai'i under early postmissionary rulers
(especially Ka-mehameha III, Ka-mehameha IV,
and Ka-mehameha V) who were accustomed to
speaking in public. They owed their training in Ha-
waiian oratory partly to what they had learned, both
systematically and unconsciously, from elder chiefs,
native guardians, and family retainers of good
background. For their facility in English Ka-me-
hameha IV, Ka-mehameha V, Luna-lilo, Ka-lā-kaua,
and Lili'u-o-ka-lani were indebted to the Chiefs'
Children's School and its Congregationalist teach-
ers. Even so, without their own sound intelligence

and initiative and capacity for leadership, formal
school exercises would probably have taught them
very little.

Queen Emma, who at one time attended the
school, but who was also educated by private tutors,
had definite ideas about the training of political
leaders. In a letter to her leper cousin, Peter Kaeo,
January 6, 1874, she gives Peter advice on how to
equip himself to return from the leper settlement
(provided he is cured) and take his rightful place
as a member of the House of Nobles in the Hawaiian
Legislature:

> During these days of your probation there, dear Peter,
> be ambitious and bold to hold our ancestral renown ever
> in its place high. Let not inferiors step into our places.
> Speak and act with authority where you are at present.
> Speak often—either to few or many—so that by fre-
> quent practice it grows to a habit. Thus you perfect your-
> self to public speaking besides accomplishing our end,
> which is bringing these people to look to and lean on you
> as the head mover in all things.
>
> You see an illustration of all this in Taffy [David
> Ka-lā-kaua]. He has stumbled on and on to the shagrin
> [*sic*] of everybody year after year till actually now he
> claims the consideration of our entire public. He is of
> course not good. Still we cannot deny he has made a stir
> in the world, and this is what I wish you to accomplish
> also, by constantly speaking to the people of Molokai.
> Never mind whether or not the delivery is clear or your
> manner taking. At first they may even come and tell

you not to attemp [*sic*] such things again, as in Taffy's
case. Still never be discouraged. Have perseverance.
Make a name for yourself and consequently add an-
other laurel to the family tree. Help your brother
and lastly me. (Queen Emma Collection, Archives of
Hawai'i)

FEATHER CHANTS FOR QUEEN KA-PI'O-LANI

Feather chants (*mele hulu*) presented to a chief
or chiefess could be described as a subclass of
chants in praise of a chief (*mele ali'i*). As lei-songs
intended to accompany the presentation of feather
leis, and of other feathery ornaments, such chants
served as leis of affection (*mele aloha*). Elaborate
featherwork of all kinds, of course, as well as
feather cloaks, were symbols of high rank.

A feather chant could be recited either in the
kepakepa or *oli* style, depending on the atmosphere
and purpose of the occasion and the wishes and
capacities of the chanter.

THE CHERISHED ONE

Like *The Pearl*, this *oli* chant also has its stylistic
roots in the training Hawaiian rulers received from
their native counselors and helpers, especially as
this foundation was influenced by their schooling
in oratory from mission teachers and, as in the
case of Ka-mehameha IV, by Scottish, American,
and English friends. Above all, of course, was the

progress resulting from repeated practice before
audiences of many types. One point is obvious. Edu-
cation in English usage strongly affected expres-
sion in Hawaiian. In this chant the heroic references
to all eight seas, the reminder of the glorious flag
waving in the breeze, and so forth, though not the
allusions to Kumu-kāhi and Lehua, might well be
translations into Hawaiian from a written-and-
memorized exercise at the Chiefs' Children's School
in the 1840s.

THE SPRINKLER

Hawaiians of the nineteenth century must have
composed thousands of humorous songs and ditties
—*mele hoʻomākeʻaka*, literally, 'funny songs'. Most
of them have been forgotten. Despite the novelty
of its major images, at first reading so untradi-
tional, *The Sprinkler* is a delightful lesson in some
highly traditional qualities of the Hawaiian lan-
guage. The invention of the word *wiliwiliwai*, 'lawn
sprinkler' is an utterly natural extension of the
verb form *wiliwili*, a reduplication of *wili*, as in
pā wiliwili 'blowing of wind in all directions'. The
word for 'light, moving rain', *koʻiawe*, is common
in the old poetry both as a fact of weather and as
an allusion to love or lovemaking. The beautiful
word *mālie* 'calm, quiet, still, gentle', as in *"Mālie
ke kai me ka makani,"* 'the sea and wind are calm'

appears again and again musically in the lyric
descriptions of Pele and Hiʻi-aka. On examination
The Sprinkler seems to interweave terms from tra-
ditional life with their extended meanings as de-
rived from town society of the 1880s and 1890s
and as carried on into the new century. Despite the
permutations, including the suggestion of hula-
girl coquettishness in the song, its foundation in
the ancient art should not be minimized. Liliʻu-
o-ka-lani saluting the McKibbin sprinkler from
her own gardens at Washington Place is not wholly
alienated from Hiʻi-aka apostrophizing tufts of
lily buds in an Oʻahu swamp or wondering with
what gift she should celebrate the steep-gullied
streams of Ka-ʻena where they trickle down to the
sea.

    The Sprinkler is sometimes performed today as a
dance. The choral effects, sung in a Western style, with
male and female voices counterposed, may have
evolved in the transformation of the *mele* through
various stages and types of hula performance.

PELE RAPED

    As noted earlier, the selection is based on an
excerpt from Emerson's Hawaiian text for the long
chant, the *mele hula*, of Malae-haʻa-koa, in chap-
ter 23, "The Lame Fisherman: His Epic Recital
Celebrating Pele." Elsewhere, in his index, Emerson

lists the chant as an "*oli* by Malae-haʻa-koa and
his wife." In his narrative prose link in chapter
23, Emerson mentions that the chant was accom-
panied by dancing:

> Malae-Haʻa-koa and his wife stood forth and led in the
> performance of a sacred dance, accompanying their
> rhythmic motions with a long mele that recited the
> deeds, the events, the mysteries that had marked Pele's
> reign since the establishment of her dominion in
> Hawaii.

Apart from the mode of presentation described
in Emerson's book, Hawaiians themselves prob-
ably performed the chant sometimes as an *oli* with-
out dancing and sometimes as a chanted hula with
dance accompaniment. In any event, the sequence
of epic and lyric sections that make up the chant as
a whole must have been a challenge to the finest of
nineteenth-century performers, indeed to chanters
and dancers of any period. The composition was
possibly known to certain *kumu hula* as late as the
reign of Ka-lā-kaua. A text and translation, densely
sprinkled with textual variants from Emerson's
version, was published under the title *Prayer of
Malae-haʻa-koa,* in the *Fornander Collection of
Hawaiian Antiquities and Folklore,* Memoirs of
the Bernice Pauahi Bishop Museum, vol. 6, part 3
(Honolulu, 1920), pp. 492–498. This complex

work deserves systematic comparative study, drawing upon Hawaiian newspaper resources. Until this is accomplished, pronouncements on many aspects of the chant are risky.

RAMBLE ROUND HAWAI'I

A chant for a string figure game was called a *mele hei* (literally, 'net song'). The word *hei* can also mean "adept, deft; to absorb, as knowledge or skill," suggesting that in a string game, when played cleverly, it is possible to ensnare knowledge and explore it pleasantly.

BEHOLD

The song, a *mele hula*, was composed in the early 1930s by Mrs. Pukui together with her mother, Pa'ana Wiggin, during a period when Mrs. Pukui was teaching Hawaiian stories, traditions, dances, and songs in primary classes at Punahou School in Honolulu. On one occasion, when Mrs. Pukui became ill and could not meet a class, Mrs. Wiggin, herself a dancer and daughter of a dancer, took over as substitute teacher. A photograph of the period shows Mrs. Wiggin, a tall Hawaiian lady in a white *holokū*, teaching the song to a group of youngsters on the Punahou lawn. Pele Pukui, Mrs. Wiggin's very young granddaughter, is about to demonstrate with stick-dance movements and gestures the four directions—*luna, lalo, mauka, makai*—illustrated in this sitting hula song. The verses have been included in another translation, under the title *The Beautiful*, in a recent outstanding anthology for children, edited by Richard Lewis: *Out of the Earth I Sing: Poetry and Songs of the Primitive Peoples of the World* (New York: W. W. Norton, 1968).

Bibliography

The following is a list of the chief books and articles consulted in preparing this anthology; in particular, sources that have provided printed texts for translations or that have been directly quoted in commentaries.

Beckwith, Martha Warren. *Hawaiian Mythology.* New Haven: Yale University Press, 1940. Reprint. Honolulu: University of Hawaii Press, 1970.
———. "Hawaiian Shark Aumakua." *American Anthropologist* 19 (1917) : 503–517.
———. *The Kumulipo: A Hawaiian Creation Chant.* Chicago: University of Chicago Press, 1951. Reprint. Honolulu: The University Press of Hawaii, 1972.
Daws, Gavan. *Shoal of Time: A History of the Hawaiian Islands.* New York: Macmillan Co., 1968.
Elbert, Samuel H., and Samuel A. Keala. *Conversational Hawaiian.* 5th ed. Honolulu: University of Hawaii Press, 1965.
Elbert, Samuel H., and Noelani Mahoe. *Nā Mele o Hawaiʻi Nei: 101 Hawaiian Songs.* Honolulu: University of Hawaii Press, 1970.
Emerson, Nathaniel B. *Pele and Hiʻiaka, A Myth of Hawaii.* Honolulu: Honolulu Star-Bulletin, 1915.
———. *Unwritten Literature: The Sacred Songs of the Hula.* Washington, D. C.: Bureau of American Ethnology Bulletins, No. 38, 1909. Reprint. Rutland, Vermont and Tokyo, Japan: Charles E. Tuttle Co., 1965.
Finney, Ben R., and James D. Houston. *Surfing: The Sport*

of Hawaiian Kings. Rutland, Vermont and Tokyo, Japan: Charles E. Tuttle Co., 1966.

Handy, Edward S. C., *Cultural Revolution in Hawaii*. New York: Institute of Pacific Relations, 1931.

Handy, Edward S. C., Mary Kawena Pukui, and Elizabeth Green Handy. *The Polynesian Family System in Ka'u, Hawaii*. Wellington, New Zealand: The Polynesian Society, Reprint No. 6, 1958.

"Hawaiian Sugar Plantation History: No. 17—Waimanalo, Island of Hawaii." Honolulu Star-Bulletin, June 22, 1935.

Ii, John Papa. *Fragments of Hawaiian History*. Translated by Mary Kawena Pukui. Edited by Dorothy B. Barrere. Honolulu: Bishop Museum Press, 1963.

Kahananui, Dorothy M. *Music of Ancient Hawaii: A Brief Survey*. Honolulu: privately printed, 1960, 1962.

Kamakau, Samuel M. *Ruling Chiefs of Hawaii*. Honolulu: The Kamehameha Schools, 1961.

———. *Ka Po'e Kahiko: The People of Old*. Translated by Mary Kawena Pukui. Edited by Dorothy B. Barrere. Honolulu: Bishop Museum Press, 1964.

Korn, Alfons L. *The Victorian Visitors*. Honolulu: University of Hawaii Press, 1958. Reprint, 1969.

Kuykendall, Ralph S. "An Hawaiian in Mexico." *Hawaiian Historical Society Report* (1923): 37–50.

———. *The Hawaiian Kingdom: 1874–1893: The Kalakaua Dynasty*. Vol. 3. Honolulu: University of Hawaii Press, 1967.

Luomala, Katharine. *Voices on the Wind: Polynesian Myths and Chants*. Honolulu: Bishop Museum Press, 1959.

Malo, David. *Hawaiian Antiquities (Moolelo Hawaii)*. Translated (1898) by Nathaniel B. Emerson. Bishop Museum Special Publications, no. 2. Honolulu: Bishop Museum Press, 1951.

McAllister, J. Gilbert. *The Archaeology of Oahu*. Bernice

P. Bishop Museum Bulletin 104. Honolulu: Bishop
Museum Press, 1933.

Poignant, Roslyn. *Oceanic Mythology: The Myths of
Polynesia, Micronesia, Melanesia, Australia.* London: Paul Hamlyn, 1967.

Pukui, Mary Kawena. "Songs (meles) of Old Ka'u,
Hawaii." *Journal of American Folklore* 62 (1949):
247–258.

Pukui, Mary Kawena, and Samuel H. Elbert. *Hawaiian
Dictionary.* Honolulu: University of Hawaii Press,
1971.

————. *Place Names of Hawaii.* Honolulu: University of
Hawaii Press, 1966.

Roberts, Helen H. *Ancient Hawaiian Music.* Bishop Museum Bulletin No. 29. Honolulu: Bishop Museum
Press, 1926. Reprint. New York: Dover Publications, 1967.

Rothenberg, Jerome. *Technicians of the Sacred: A Range
of Poetries from America, Asia and Oceania.* New
York: Doubleday and Co., 1968.

Sterling, Elspeth P., and Catherine C. Summers. *The Sites
of Oahu.* Honolulu: Bishop Museum Press, 1964.

Thompson, Laura. *The Secret of Culture: Nine Community Studies.* New York: Random House, 1969.

Winne, Jane Lathrop, and Mary Kawena Pukui. *'Olelo
No'eau A Ka Hawai'i: Folk Sayings from the
Hawaiian.* Honolulu: 1961.